BISMARCK AND BRITISH COLONIAL POLICY

BISMARCK

BISMARCK
AND
BRITISH COLONIAL POLICY

The Problem of South West Africa
1883–1885

By
WILLIAM OSGOOD AYDELOTTE

NEGRO UNIVERSITIES PRESS
WESTPORT, CONNECTICUT

Originally published in 1937
by University of Pennsylvania Press, Philadelphia

Reprinted in 1970 by
Negro Universities Press
A Division of Greenwood Press, Inc.
Westport, Connecticut

Library of Congress Catalogue Card Number 71-111563

SBN 8371-4584-8

Printed in the United States of America

PREFACE

THE resurgence of imperialism in the last third of the nineteenth century was perhaps the most important political movement of the era preceding the World War. In the 1850's the impulse to acquire oversea possessions and establish colonies had almost wholly died down, both in England and on the continent of Europe. But even in this period the seeds of the new imperialism, economic needs and popular enthusiasms, were beginning to develop and, in the five decades that followed, the imperialist movement sprang up, hesitantly at first, then with increasing force until it reached a climax about the turn of the century. In the 1870's and 1880's the movement got under way: Italy and Belgium entered the colonial field, France continued in it, Russia pursued her expansion eastward, England began to add to her already great possessions, and in 1884 Germany joined in the scramble for the lands still unappropriated.

Germany's colonial history was in several ways unique. It was shorter than that of any other great power: Germany was the last country to enter the colonial field and, because of the Treaty of Versailles, the first to leave it. Besides this, Germany never got so much or such valuable territory as did most of the other countries, partly because of her tardiness and partly because Bismarck, under whom Germany acquired her first colonies, was himself a lukewarm expansionist and, after his first effort, did not prosecute his policy of annexation energetically. But although the German colonial empire was never of major importance in size or in production of wealth, it acquired a different kind of importance through the fact that Germany was in 1884 the leading country of Europe. Indeed, the really significant thing about the German colonial departure was the consequences which it had for international politics. Its immediate result was to cause an acrid dispute between England and Germany. For the future it created a field in which British and German interests closely touched and where conflicts were likely to arise. Looking further ahead, it is now clear that Bismarck's adoption of a colonial program was the first signal for a new orientation of German policy. To Bismarck colonies were a side issue. But in the hands of his less discriminating successors his half-hearted colonial policy was transmuted into an interest in and a desire to participate in political affairs all over the world. In this sense Bismarck, perhaps unwittingly, paved the way for the *Weltpolitik* of later years and the naval rivalry with England. With the colonial demands of the present National Socialist Government the story has entered still another phase.

This book deals with the first chapter in the history of the German colonial empire, the dispute between Germany and England over South West Africa during the years 1883-85. This topic has for many reasons a peculiar significance. Since South West Africa was the first German colony, its history shows most clearly the reactions and readjustments both in British and German policy which were the consequence of the German colonial program. The incident also brings into relief several great political trends of the late nineteenth century: the growth of imperialism in Germany and in England, the conflict in the latter country between the different systems of colonial thought, the diplomatic problem of conducting negotiations between a democratic and an autocratic state, and the causes and results of these two different methods of diplomacy. Above all the story furnishes a superb illustration of Bismarck's diplomatic technique.

Because of its special importance, the South West African controversy will be treated in some detail. Only the exhaustive, says a distinguished modern writer, can be truly interesting. This is the interest which is sought here. The attempt has been made to present not a general survey of the period but a description of specific events. At the same time, the German colonial question is closely bound up with other circumstances, and it has been necessary to go well outside the bare details of the negotiations in order to explain all the influences at work on British and German policy. For this reason a good deal of space has been given in the first two chapters to the colonial and political background in both England and Germany, and especially to the way in which this background affected the men in office in 1883-85. On the other hand, less attention has been given to those subjects which have been adequately discussed elsewhere. The Egyptian problem and the general diplomatic situation at the time have been admirably handled in recent books, and there was no reason to go over ground which had already been covered. Full consideration has, however, been given to these factors both in the narrative and in the conclusions.

This study is based largely on unpublished documents. To the scholar, one of the special attractions of the South West African controversy is that it has only recently become possible to tell the whole story. There are large gaps in the Blue Books and White Books issued by the two governments at the time, and these gaps are by no means fully covered by subsequent publications of documents in *Die Grosse Politik*, the life of Lord Granville and elsewhere. With all these published sources a great deal was still not clear, particularly on the German side. The materials for this book have been taken from the archives of the British foreign office in London, the German foreign office in Berlin, and the private papers of Mr. Gladstone and the second Earl Granville. This examination of the documents now makes it possible to tell the story in a new light and to suggest several additions to what has hitherto been known. The conclusions to which this fuller information leads are set forth in Chapter VII.

The author wishes to express his thanks to the authorities of the Public Record Office and the British Museum in London and the German foreign office and the Reichsarchiv in Berlin. He is indebted to the *Cambridge Historical Journal* for permission to republish certain portions of this book appearing therein. Thanks are also due to Mr. A. Tilney Bassett for his assistance with the Gladstone Papers, and to Professor William E. Lingelbach of the University of Pennsylvania, who was kind enough to read the book in manuscript and has made a number of valuable suggestions. To Professor Harold Temperley of Cambridge University the book owes a debt greater than can be expressed.

W. O. A.

Swarthmore, Pa.

CONTENTS

Page

PREFACE v

CHAPTER

I. The Situation in England 1

II. Bismarck Opens the Negotiations 18

III. The British Reception of Bismarck's Inquiries 40

IV. Münster's Mission 59

V. Count Herbert Bismarck's Mission 89

VI. The Final Negotiations 113

VII. Conclusion 125

APPENDIX I. Joseph Chamberlain and the Majuba Crisis 137

APPENDIX II. A Critical Examination of the British Blue Books and German White Book on South West Africa 142

APPENDIX III. Count Herbert Bismarck 154

APPENDIX IV. Gladstone's Position on the German Colonial Question 163

BIBLIOGRAPHY 169

INDEX 177

ILLUSTRATIONS

BISMARCK *frontispiece*

"Spy" in *Vanity Fair,* October 15, 1870

THE CABINET COUNCIL *facing page* 14

"T." in *Vanity Fair,* November 27, 1883

COUNT MÜNSTER *facing page* 82

"Spy" in *Vanity Fair,* December 23, 1876

EARL GRANVILLE *facing page* 130

"Spy" in *Vanity Fair,* March 13, 1869

NOTE

Signs in the text refer to notes at the bottom of the pages; Arabic numbers refer to notes at the end of each chapter.

The full titles of all sources cited in the notes will be found in the Bibliography.

I

THE SITUATION IN ENGLAND

FROM the beginning of the British occupation of Egypt in 1882 until the early months of 1884 the relations between Germany and England were of the most amicable character. The occupation of Egypt had plunged England into a host of international difficulties. France, who up to that time had collaborated with England in Egypt, refused to participate in an armed intervention, and was thus changed from an ally into a critic. England's only support in Europe was Prince Bismarck, chancellor of the German Empire, who, during the trying first two years of the British occupation, acted with tact and friendliness, and avoided in every way making difficulties for the British Government. His attitude was appreciated in England, and several of the British ministers expressed their thanks in very definite terms.

The relations between the two countries were further improved by a personal factor, highly important in this case. In the last months of 1881 Prince Bismarck placed his eldest son, Count Herbert Bismarck, in London in a temporary position at the German embassy. Lord Granville, the British foreign secretary, acting on urgent hints from the British ambassador in Berlin, gave Herbert Bismarck a magnificent reception, in spite of warnings from the German Crown Princess, Queen Victoria's daughter, who was strongly anti-Bismarck. Granville's cordiality encouraged Prince Bismarck, as he confided to the British ambassador, Lord Ampthill, to appoint his son to the post of first secretary of embassy in London. Count Herbert Bismarck remained, and continued to enjoy the pleasures of the London season (1). He wrote to Count Plessen: "I have been pampered in London as I have never yet been in my life. I cannot picture to myself a more delightful society."* Prince Bismarck was also greatly pleased, and he asked Lord Ampthill to thank Lord and Lady Granville for their "immense kindness" to Herbert, and "said he never could be sufficiently grateful for the reception his son had met with in England."† All this time, the good relations between Germany and England continued to improve. "Never," Lord Ampthill wrote privately to Granville, "was your kindness politically better invested, and I chuckle in my sleeve when I hear people marvel at Bismarck's growing preference for England and steady faith in the foreign policy of Her Majesty's Liberal advisers."‡

But in 1884 the situation changed completely. The support which Bismarck had been giving to England in Egypt suddenly stopped, and the relations between the two countries became extremely difficult. The cause of the estrangement was the dispute over South West Africa, the first German colony.

In this dispute the British Government pursued a policy which entirely alienated Bismarck and incurred the bitter criticism of a large section of the British press and public opinion. The surprising feature of the incident was that the object pursued by Bismarck, of German colonization, was not one which the leading British statesmen were naturally inclined to oppose. Most of the senior members of the English cabinet, such as Gladstone, Derby, and Selborne, as well as Harcourt and Northbrook, believed that England's colonial responsibilities were already great enough, and that it was undesirable to make fresh annexations. The views of some of these men were altered in the course of time, and there were undoubtedly imperialistic influences at work in the cabinet. But it seems to have been accepted as a fact by members of the British Government that German colonization would not seriously conflict with British objects. Yet in spite

* Wolfgang Windelband: *Herbert Bismarck als Mitarbeiter seines Vaters,* p. 11.

† 25 March 1882. Lord Ampthill to Lord Granville. Lord Edmond Fitzmaurice: *Life of Lord Granville,* II, 257.

‡ 3 February 1883. Lord Ampthill to Lord Granville. Private. Private Granville MSS, G.D. 29/178.

of this recognition, a bitter dispute occurred. One reason for this dispute was that Bismarck was dealing with a system of diplomacy completely different from his own. The peculiarities of British foreign policy, though they were inherent in the principles of the British constitution, had not been so much in evidence during the first years of the Liberal administration, when the relations with Germany were comparatively friendly. The dispute over Angra Pequena brought them out.

The difference between German and British diplomacy was fundamental, and was due to the difference between the systems of government of these two countries. The successful establishment of conservatism in Germany had given Bismarck a control over foreign affairs that was almost absolute. The singleness of authority governing German diplomacy, as well as the secrecy with which this diplomacy could be conducted, enabled Bismarck to pursue an elaborate and subtle policy which would have been impossible for a differently constituted state. In England it was otherwise. There the direction of foreign affairs was anything but authoritative. For a really important measure of policy, it was necessary to secure the approval of a large group of men who frequently differed widely in their opinions. In foreign affairs this method of procedure was a serious impediment. Lord Salisbury, who realized the situation clearly, described it in the following terms: "There is much else that weakens our diplomacy—our shifting foreign policy during the last ten years—our precarious Governments, the necessity of adapting our foreign policy to the views of a Cabinet of fourteen or sixteen men, usually ignorant of it and seldom united in their views."* The difficulties which Salisbury described were particularly aggravated in the case of Angra Pequena. A strong foreign secretary, who knew what should be done and could carry the cabinet with him, would perhaps have been able to remedy matters, but Lord Granville permitted himself

* 29 August 1886. The Marquis of Salisbury to Queen Victoria. G. E. Buckle: *Letters of Queen Victoria,* 3rd Series, I, 195.

to be guided by other members of the cabinet only too freely. Not only did the different British ministers desire different things, but certain of them, and even certain parts of the empire whose interests were concerned, were allowed to exercise an unfortunate influence upon foreign affairs. On one occasion, when Bismarck addressed an urgent inquiry to the British foreign office, the matter was referred to the colonial office, which in turn referred it to one of the colonial governments, so that it was six months before Bismarck finally received an answer.

Such a method of proceeding was perhaps justified, in consideration of the theory of cabinet responsibility and in consideration of the independence of the great British colonial communities, but it was extremely irritating to Bismarck, who refused to admit that it was anything more than an evasion. He wrote to Münster, his ambassador in London: "It is the same as though, supposing the French complained about the conduct of the Reichsland Government, we were to refer to the independent status of the local administration and the territorial representatives."* This is, of course, not a true parallel, since the British Government, according to its constitution, was bound to give consideration to the wishes of the self-governing colonies in matters that affected their interests. But, even so, the joint control of a large body of men over foreign affairs, as well as the loose construction of the British Empire, engendered a lack of formality which was deeply repugnant to the Prussian character. When Bismarck refused to permit the German ambassador to confer with the British colonial secretary, even though the latter was declared to know more about the matter in question than the foreign secretary, the chancellor was not merely taking a stand of rigid formality which was very convenient at the moment for practical reasons, but he was falling back on the traditions of Prussian diplomacy. The direct control that Bismarck exercised over foreign affairs, and the subtlety and refinement

* 1 June 1884. Prince Bismarck to Count Münster. E. T. S. Dugdale: *German Diplomatic Documents, 1871–1914*, I, 176.

of his methods, naturally brought about a sharpness of detail and a punctiliousness in the forms of diplomatic intercourse which was completely alien to British practice.

The confusion resulting from the devious ways of British diplomacy was still further increased in this case by the lack of unanimity among the members of the British Government regarding the advantage of colonies. If Lord Derby was in favor of concessions to the greed of the Australian colonists, there were other members of the government who did not agree with him, and who held that the empire was already large enough, without fresh annexations. Others still were strong imperialists. By 1883, in fact, the anti-imperialism and indifference to colonial affairs which characterized the first part of the Victorian era were already things of the past. In the late 'sixties and early 'seventies new influences had begun to make themselves felt. The growth of industrialism on the continent and the general shift from free trade to protection already threatened to endanger the economic supremacy of England and to deprive her of some of her former markets. The reaction towards imperialism was further stimulated by the attempts of the other powers to acquire colonies, and by the reaction in England towards national self-assertiveness and Jingoism which did so much to put the Disraeli administration into power in 1874.* But this reaction, vigorous as it was, did not carry everybody along with it. In individual cases anti-imperialism survived the defeat, and, however the younger men might be inclined, many of the older Liberals in the cabinet of 1880-85 still kept to the belief which they had held for the greater part of their careers.

This was especially true in the case of Gladstone. "Throughout the whole of my political life," he declared in 1882, "whether under Sir Robert Peel or as a Member of the Liberal Party, I cannot recollect an occasion on which I gave a vote or took a step in a controverted matter except on the the side which was opposed to annexation."† Gladstone

* C. A. Bodelsen: *Studies in Mid-Victorian Imperialism,* pp. 79, 87.

† 17 March 1882. *Hansard Parliamentary Debates,* 3rd Series, CCLXVII, 1190.

was greatly interested in colonies, but, while he realized their material advantages, he cared much more about their moral and social value. He criticized his opponents because they discovered the chief value of colonies in "the administrative connection, and the shadow of political subordination."* He himself visualized England's colonial mission very differently. It was, as he saw it, to create free independent communities in all parts of the globe, who would enjoy the inestimable benefit of English institutions. He recalled with approbation Roebuck's expression, "that the object of colonization is the creation of so many happy Englands." This lofty conception of the purposes of colonization colored his views upon the acquisition of territory. He resolutely opposed all attempts at aggrandizement which did not conduce to these purposes. He asserted that mere extension of territory was not a legitimate object of ambition, "unless you can show that you are qualified to make use of that territory for the purposes for which God gave the earth to man."† He believed passionately in self-determination, and declared in the House of Commons that: "So far as it was possible to lay down an abstract and general rule with regard to annexation, he was prepared to say that Her Majesty's Government would not annex any territory, great or small, without the well-understood and expressed wish of the people to be annexed, freely and generously expressed, and authenticated by the best means the case would afford."‡

Gladstone's view was that the burden of empire was already too heavy, "the Government were overwhelmed and totally inadequate to undertake their own responsibilities . . . from year to year the Government were groaning over the mass of work left undone,"§ and he thought that additions to the empire were a source of increased expenditure

* W. E. Gladstone: *England's Mission,* in the *Nineteenth Century,* September 1878, p. 571.

† 12 November 1855. W. E. Gladstone: *Our Colonies,* a speech at Chester, quoted in Paul Knaplund: *Gladstone and Britain's Imperial Policy,* pp. 198–99.

‡ 25 June 1872. *Hansard Parliamentary Debates,* 3rd Series, CCXII, 217.

§ 25 June 1872. *Hansard Parliamentary Debates,* 3rd Series, CCXII, 215–16.

but not of strength. "I should be glad to know," he wrote, "whether the Belgian Government and people, who naturally lean upon us more than on any other Power, contemplate, with the same satisfaction as our Imperialists, the mode now in fashion of strengthening England by giving her plenty to do all over the world, and no means of doing it."*

Gladstone found some sympathy for his views among the senior members of the cabinet. Lord Derby, the colonial secretary, was personally inclined against imperialism and annexation, although he was influenced by public opinion and by pressure from the colonies. Northbrook, the First Lord of the Admiralty, shared Derby's natural inclinations (2). Lord Selborne, the Lord Chancellor, took a great interest in the welfare of native peoples, and had "a very strong feeling against the tendency of European nations to appropriate and occupy countries inhabited by uncivilized or imperfectly civilized races, as if their inhabitants had no rights. . . ."† Besides these, there was Sir William Harcourt, the home secretary, whose life-long hostility to imperialism is described by his biographer as "perhaps the most deeply rooted political motive of his career."‡ But Gladstone met with opposition from the two radical members of the cabinet, Sir Charles Dilke and Joseph Chamberlain, who, each in a different way, represented the new imperialism.

Dilke marks the intermediate stage between the anti-colonial and the imperialist schools of English colonial thought in the Victorian era. His interest in colonial matters was great, and he believed that England had an important colonial mission, which was the creation of great democratic communities with English institutions. The English race, in the form of these communities, would, he believed, one day dominate the earth. In the preface to a book describing his journeys through English-speaking countries, he wrote: "The idea which in all the length of my travels has been at once

* W. E. Gladstone: *England's Mission*, in the *Nineteenth Century*, September 1878, p. 574.

† Earl of Selborne: *Memorials*, II, 103.

‡ A. G. Gardiner: *Life of Sir William Harcourt*, I, 47.

my fellow and my guide—a key wherewith to unlock the hidden things of strange new lands—is a conception, however imperfect, of the grandeur of our race, already girdling the earth, which it is destined, perhaps, eventually to overspread."* Dilke later referred to this preface as "the best piece of work of my life. It states the doctrine on which our rule should be based—remembered in Canada—forgotten in South Africa—the true as against the bastard Imperialism."† But Dilke was a cosmopolitan, and it is important to note that his rather arrogant confidence was placed not in his country, but in the English race as a whole. That the inevitable triumph of Saxondom would consist in the universal domination of England, Dilke neither imagined nor hoped. "The ultimate future of any one section of our race, however, is of little moment by the side of its triumph as a whole, but the power of English laws and English principles of government is not merely an English question—its continuance is essential to the freedom of mankind."‡ Dilke concluded that, since the self-governing colonies were of almost no value for the purposes of commerce, emigration, or military power, their separation from the mother country was a harmless procedure, though it was not especially to be desired.§ His separatism, it must be added, greatly diminished in the course of time.||

But Dilke held very different views on the crown colonies and India. In regard to these he was never a separatist at all, in fact very much the opposite. Unlike Chamberlain, he placed the crown colonies (which he called "dependencies")¶ first and the self-governing colonies second, in their value for England. Although, for the most part, the dependencies were not suitable for emigration, they had considerable use for trading purposes. In their case, trade actually did follow the

* Sir Charles W. Dilke: *Greater Britain,* p. vii.
† Gwynn and Tuckwell: *Life of Sir Charles W. Dilke,* I, 68.
‡ Sir Charles W. Dilke: *Greater Britain,* p. 565.
§ *Ibid.,* pp. 385–91.
|| Sir Charles W. Dilke: *Problems of Greater Britain,* pp. 695–96.
¶ Sir Charles W. Dilke: *Greater Britain,* pp. 385–86.

flag. For if England were to leave Australia or the Cape, she would continue to be the chief customer of these countries, but "were we to leave India or Ceylon, they would have no customers at all; for, falling into anarchy, they would cease at once to export their goods to us and to consume our manufactures."*

The territories which Germany annexed were inhabited chiefly by uncivilized natives, they were as yet unfit for self-government, and hence, if England had annexed them, it could only have been as crown colonies. Dilke was always in favor of crown colonies, and his earlier opinion was still maintained when he became a member of the Gladstone administration. When, in 1882, two native chiefs in the Cameroons proposed to be taken under British protection, Dilke pressed for the acceptance of their offer.† He wrote: "I have read up the literature of the Cameroons. After reading Captain Burton's report made in 1862 I am strongly of opinion that the offer of the two kings to Mr. Gladstone should not be refused without enquiry."‡ Many of the lands taken by Bismarck had been previously refused by England, and Dilke felt that, in view of the differential duties imposed by other powers on British goods, this refusal was "founded upon old-fashioned grounds unfortunately inapplicable to the circumstances of the day."§ He was none too pleased when Bismarck seized the Cameroons,‖ though after the event he admitted that a German annexation was "not a bad thing for us" and was "preferable to a French" annexation, since the Germans did not impose such heavy duties as the French.¶ But tariffs were generally increasing, and Dilke realized this and saw the value of tropical dependencies for commercial

* Sir Charles W. Dilke: *Greater Britain*, pp. 553–57.

† Gwynn and Tuckwell: *Life of Sir Charles W. Dilke*, II, 83.

‡ 13 January 1882. Minute by Sir Charles W. Dilke. Private Granville MSS, G.D. 29/122.

§ Sir Charles W. Dilke: *The Present Position of European Politics*, pp. 53–54.

‖ 28 August 1884. Dilke to Chamberlain. J. L. Garvin: *Life of Joseph Chamberlain*, I, 495.

¶ Sir Charles W. Dilke: *The Present Position of European Politics*, pp. 54–55.

purposes. He believed in a vigorous foreign policy based on large armaments,* and he usually favored strong British action against the annexations of Bismarck.

It is not altogether easy to say what were Joseph Chamberlain's views on imperialism at this early stage in his life. In Gladstone's second ministry, when Chamberlain was president of the Board of Trade, his contact with questions of colonial policy was only indirect. It is even difficult to say whether he was an imperialist at all at this time. The arguments he advanced, on matters where the question of imperialism might enter in, were for the most part not based upon statements of the general desirability of annexation or upon imperialistic principles of any kind.

He was a violent opponent of the annexation of the Transvaal. He voted against it in 1877, he pressed for its reversal when he came into office in 1880, and when the Transvaal was given back most of its independence in 1881 he vigorously defended the policy of the government in the House of Commons and in public. But in his whole discussion of the Transvaal, Chamberlain hardly mentioned the questions of imperialism and annexation at all. The point seems rather to have been that Chamberlain was at this time not so much interested in acquiring territory, but, as a good radical, was very much interested in putting into effect the principle of self-determination and in making the inhabitants of a country run their own affairs.†

At no point in the early part of his career did Chamberlain come out strongly in favor of annexation. It is true that he had few occasions on which to give expression to his views on colonial subjects. But when he did touch such subjects, his arguments ran for the most part on other lines. In Egypt he was interested chiefly in considerations of prestige. So firm was his stand on this point that he earned in some quarters the reputation of a Jingo,‡ a charge which he vigorously

* 10 June 1898. Speech by Dilke. Quoted in Gwynn and Tuckwell: *Life of Sir Charles W. Dilke,* II, 494-95.

† See Appendix I.

‡ December 1882. John Bright to George Dixon. G. M. Trevelyan: *Life of John Bright,* p. 435.

denied. He was, indeed, not in favor of a permanent occupation of that country. "But I have never changed my mind," he wrote to Morley, "that, having intervened, it is our business to come away as quickly as we possibly can."* Chamberlain attempted to distinguish between Jingoism and standing up for England's actual rights. He declared he was for a peaceful and non-aggressive policy, but insisted that England's rights and interests must be protected under all circumstances. He was by no means an advocate of "peace at any price."

His attitude in regard to the German colonies was a similar one. The issue which was predominant in his mind was prestige, not imperialism. He objected not so much to what Bismarck did as to the manner in which it was done.† He admitted England could not set up a colonial monopoly. "If foreign nations," he said, "are determined to pursue distant colonial enterprises, we have no right to prevent them. We cannot anticipate them in every case by proclaiming a universal protectorate. . . . "‡ At the same time he was well aware of the potential value to England of some of the territories Bismarck acquired, such as the Cameroons.§ But the point on which he laid most stress was prestige. He was willing to let Germany have colonies, but he was not willing to let Bismarck bully England in the process of getting them.

In the year 1883 the views of the members of the cabinet were tested and clarified, and the questions of annexation and imperialism were brought into especial prominence by the attempts of Australia to annex the island of New Guinea. In the spring of 1883, the government of Queensland announced that, subject to the approval of the home government, they had annexed the whole of that part of New Guinea which was unoccupied by the Dutch. This announce-

* 31 March 1883. Chamberlain to John Morley. J. L. Garvin: *Life of Joseph Chamberlain,* I, 501.

† 29 December 1884. Chamberlain to Dilke. J. L. Garvin: *Life of Joseph Chamberlain,* I, 497-98.

‡ 5 January 1885. Speech by Chamberlain at Birmingham. Henry W. Lucy: *Speeches of Joseph Chamberlain,* p. 103.

§ 12 September 1884. Chamberlain to Dilke. J. L. Garvin: *Life of Joseph Chamberlain,* I, 495.

ment had a great effect in England, on public opinion as well as in governmental circles. Lord Carnarvon, a typical imperialist, wrote a letter to the *Morning Post* urging the Liberal government "to consent to the inevitable, and above all to consent to it graciously."* Even Mr. T. B. Potter, M.P., of the Cobden Club, wrote to Lord Derby on 18 May 1883 saying: "I am no advocate for annexation as a rule but I am not sure that in the present case it may not be a wise step." Derby, who was inclined to be guided by public opinion, sent the letter on to Gladstone with the comment: "Mr. Potter as you know is the Cobden Club—the life and soul of it. I did not expect to find him on the side of annexation anywhere, and his going with the popular feeling shows how strong it must be."†

Selborne's reaction to the Queensland annexation was a very emphatic one. He wrote to Gladstone: "I am, at present, unable to conceive, that any necessity, or justification, for taking *the whole* of that immense country (or what the Dutch have not already taken,) *can* be made out: and I should consider such an act impolitic in a very high degree, and also morally unjustifiable, if it were done without demonstrable necessity, and without that sort of invitation and concurrence, on the part of the principal native tribes or their Rulers, which we had in the case of Fiji."‡ Gladstone replied, expressing his hearty sympathy and concurrence, and sent Selborne's letter on to Lord Derby (3). But the latter was doubtful. "I have no love for annexations," he wrote back, "any more than the Lord Chancellor; but I imagine that Australia will be unanimous on this question, and we must be careful not give [sic] more offence there than we can help."§

In this case, Mr. Gladstone was completely successful, and he was able to report to the Queen on 13 June 1883 that the

* 12 July 1883. Sir Arthur Hardinge: *Life of Lord Carnarvon,* III, 122-23.
† 26 May 1883. Lord Derby to Mr. Gladstone. Private Gladstone MSS.
‡ 22 April 1883. Lord Selborne to Mr. Gladstone. Private Gladstone MSS.
§ 23 April 1883. Lord Derby to Mr. Gladstone. Private Gladstone MSS.

cabinet had decided not to confirm the so-called annexation of New Guinea by the Queensland Government.*

Baffled in the attempt to secure New Guinea by high-handed means, the Australian colonists tried another method. In December 1883 there met at Sydney an intercolonial conference, at which all the Australian colonies, New Zealand, and the Fiji Islands, were represented. This conference passed seven resolutions, of which the two perhaps most significant were as follows: "That the further acquisition of dominion in the South Pacific by any foreign power would be highly injurious to Australasia and the Empire." "That having regard to trade and other considerations, and fully recognizing that the responsibility of extending the bounds of the Empire belongs to the Imperial Government, the Conference desires the immediate incorporation of all of that part of New Guinea which is not claimed by the Dutch Government." Lord Carnarvon sympathized with these resolutions, as he had with the attempted annexation, but even for him they went a little too far. The time had perhaps come to annex the New Guinea coast, or large portions of it, but he did not see that England was yet "either compelled in self-defence, or induced by self-interest, to annex the interior of that vast and unknown territory."†

But the Australian demands appeared in a rather different light to the senior Liberal ministers. Selborne remained entirely unconvinced. "But none of the arguments which I have yet seen or heard have convinced me that such a necessity for annexing to the British Empire the whole of that part of New Guinea which has not been (nominally) annexed by the Dutch now exists."‡ Derby was more violent in his protestations but weaker in his resistance. "What can be said," he wrote, "in favor of the Monroe Doctrine laid down for

* 13 June 1883. Mr. Gladstone to Queen Victoria. G. E. Buckle: *Letters of Queen Victoria,* 2nd Series, III, 428.

† Sir Arthur Hardinge: *Life of Lord Carnarvon,* III, 125-26.

‡ Lord Selborne to Sir Henry Parkes, replying to the latter's letter of 19 November 1883. Lord Selborne: *Memorials,* II, 106–07.

the whole South Pacific? a distance of more than 5000 miles. Australia cannot be secure if any other power is allowed to establish itself between the Australian coast and South America! This is mere raving: and one can scarcely suppose it to be seriously intended: though it is hard to fix the limits of colonial self-esteem. . . . The notion that other powers, and other nationalities, may have rights which an Australian is bound to respect, does not seem to have entered the colonial mind." But whatever was Lord Derby's opinion of the justice of the Australian demands, he was very much afraid of what might happen if England did not give way to them. He did not contemplate "more than a claim formally put forward to the coast of the island so far as it is not in the hands of the Dutch. This would be enough to put an end to the fear (real or affected) of occupation by any foreign power," which was the most important thing at the moment. He added: "We could not as matters stand allow any other state to seize a part of the island: the Australians would threaten secession if we did, and everybody would be against us. . . . "*

Gladstone did not, however, agree with this account of the situation. He replied: "With the whole of the condemnatory part of your letter on the Resolutions of the Australian Convention I need hardly say that I am in absolute sympathy. This is a little qualified when I come to the affirmative part, and the New Guinea protectorate." Gladstone was doubtful about a protectorate in any circumstances, but he thought it most injudicious to raise the question of a protectorate in New Guinea as part of an answer to the "preposterous proposals of the Convention. They have supplied the best possible ground for a negative answer: and may it not be argued that it would be best to leave them to raise if they think proper the narrower question, treating their scheme for the present as one."† But Derby remained unconvinced. Although he had no personal sympathy with the extension of

* 7 December 1883. Lord Derby to Mr. Gladstone. Private. Private Gladstone MSS.

† 8 December 1883. Mr. Gladstone to Lord Derby. Copy. Private Gladstone MSS. Gladstone Letter Book, Vol. 21, p. 18.

Mr. Childers Lord Northbrook Lord Spencer Sir C. Dilke Lord Selborne Lord Hartington
Lord Carlingford Mr. Gladstone Mr. Chamberlain Sir W. V. Harcourt Mr. Dodson
Lord Granville Lord Derby Lord Kimberley

THE CABINET COUNCIL

responsibility, he was terrified by what he thought the Australians might do if England did not accede to their wishes. Seven months later he wrote to Gladstone, urging him to leave the question of a protectorate open in his replies in the House of Commons. "I am sure," wrote Derby, "that a refusal to meet what is now the wish of all Australia would have very unpleasant consequences out there: and indirectly would do much to damage us at home."*

Such was the situation in England. The cabinet, which exercised a joint responsibility and control in foreign policy, was sharply divided in its views. Gladstone, the mainstay of anti-imperialism, was opposed by Derby, whose personal reluctance to annexation had recently been much qualified by bullying from the colonists. Gladstone was supported in his opposition to annexation by Harcourt and Selborne, and occasionally by Lord Granville, but, particularly in regard to the German colonial question, he had great difficulty with the two radical ministers. Dilke and Chamberlain were in a powerful position, and when they pressed for a strong line against Germany they frequently had a majority of the cabinet with them. But, even so, they did not always prevail.

Gladstone's influence over his colleagues, though it was still great, was gradually diminishing. In 1872 he had successfully opposed the annexation of Fiji, on the ground that annexation could not be justified if the native population did not desire it. In 1881, in the case of the Transvaal, he had triumphantly asserted his principle of self-determination in spite of a bitterly opposed public opinion, and in 1883 he succeeded in suppressing the attempts of the Australians to annex New Guinea. But as the second ministry went on, Gladstone's power to get his own way diminished. His parliamentary majority, though large, could not always be controlled. It required the greatest circumspection to manage a cabinet which included both extremes of the Liberal party. The addition of Dilke, in July 1882, increased the radical and imperialist element, and Dilke's journal records more

* 31 July 1884. Lord Derby to Mr. Gladstone. Private Gladstone MSS.

than one case where Gladstone's authority was disregarded, or where he had a terrific fight to have his way. But Gladstone held out. He insisted that to maintain a control over the allocation of unoccupied territories all over the globe meant large increase of naval expenditure, and this he would not allow. The struggle went different ways at different times, and the decisions of the cabinet were often contradictory in spirit. Dilke declares that matters were frequently adjourned; when the prime minister was opposed to his cabinet. Not infrequently Gladstone got his way, but it was often with difficulty, and sometimes only after a hard fight.*

* Gwynn and Tuckwell: *Life of Sir Charles W. Dilke,* II, 82, 86.

NOTES

1. The following correspondence, which is taken from the Private Granville MSS, will illustrate the stages of Count Herbert Bismarck's first visits to London which are described in the text:

20 November 1881. Lord Ampthill to Lord Granville. Cipher telegram. G.D. 29/177.

"Personal, Private and Secret. I am told that Prince Bismarck has decided to send his eldest son as Second Secretary to the German Embassy in London and privately and personally hopes and flatters himself that it may be looked upon as a compliment by Your Lordship and by Her Majesty's Government and also as an earnest desire to wipe out the painful impression made by the scandal which unfortunately occurred last summer at the German Embassy."

26 November 1881. Lord Ampthill to Lord Granville. Private. G.D. 29/177.

". . . On the 24th Prince Bismarck wrote me a private letter asking me as a personal favour to recommend his son Herbert 'to Lord Granville's benevolence,'—to which your telegram already received enabled me to give a prompt and welcome answer.

"Prince Bismarck adores this son, who is a remarkably clever youth, and hopes to make a great statesman of him. . . ."

14 December 1881. Lord Granville to Lord Ampthill. Draft. Private. G.D. 29/206.

"You will approve of my hoping to take Herbert Bismarck out tomorrow to hunt the hare. I took him to another amusement yesterday—the meeting in Westminster Abbey where the Prince of Wales was civil to him and where I introduced him to several notabilities. All this non obstante an extract from a Berlin letter, sent to me by the Queen, describing him in very black colours. . . ."

17 December 1881. Lord Ampthill to Lord Granville. Private. G.D. 29/177.

"Prince and Princess Bismarck are deeply touched (tief gerührt) by the very great kindness you are showing their son Herbert, and I feel convinced that you will reap the benefit of it politically in the future.

"The letter you allude to describing him in very black colours was anticipated by the astute father, who knowing full well that he and his family are not in odour of sanctity in high quarters, kept Herbert's visit to England a secret at the Palace from all excepting the Emperor, until the Newspapers betrayed his arrival and called forth the letter communicated to you, after you had already been civil to him. . . ."

24 December 1881. Lord Ampthill to Lord Granville. Private. G.D. 29/177.

"Your telegram about Herbert Bismarck has made his Father and Mother so happy that the Father in his delight over it confided to me that his son was so gifted and hard working that he would make a better Ambassador than Münster if he were not too young for the Emperor to appoint him to so important a post just yet,—meanwhile your most kind reception of him encouraged the Prince to appoint him first Secretary in London whenever Stumm could be promoted to an independent Post. He was profuse in thanks to you and Lady Granville and said that Herbert wrote that 'you were the most amiable and fascinating Hosts he had ever met in his life.' I quote his own words."

31 December 1881. Lord Ampthill to Lord Granville. Private. G.D. 29/177.

"Herbert, who is enthusiastic about his visit to Walmer, leaves on Wednesday or Thursday next for England.

"Prince Bismarck, who is ambitious for his son's advancement, is especially gratified by your condescension in talking politics with so young a man. . . .

"I think you may find Herbert a useful channel to convey correct impressions to his Father with whom he is in daily correspondence."

25 February 1882. Lord Ampthill to Lord Granville. Private. G.D. 29/178.

". . . I will therefore merely say that Bismarck is pleased with our Egyptian policy and delighted at the happy letters he receives from his son Herbert from London who avows that he has never been made so much of before."

7 October 1882. Lord Ampthill to Lord Granville. Private. G.D. 29/178.

"Your kindness to Herbert has softened the fierce fond Father and taught him that Liberals are not as bad as he thought,—so much so indeed that he not only gives you his support, but also sends you back his son, as first Secretary, as soon as Stumm can be promoted to a Mission."

2. 24 October 1880. Lord Northbrook to Mr. Gladstone. Private Gladstone MSS.

". . . On Friday I have to deliver an address at Birmingham as President of the Birmingham and Midland Institute an office which I was drawn into from no fault of my own before the change of Government.

"I am going to talk to them about the Natives of India, and although I shall not touch upon Afghan policy it is only natural to deliver something against annexations and for peace and economy—in fact to try to give a strong anti-Jingo moral to the address. . . ."

3. 23 April 1883. Mr. Gladstone to Lord Selborne. Copy. Private Gladstone MSS.

"I send your letter *re* New Guinea on to Lord Derby: having read it with much sympathy and concurrence. It will take a great deal to convince me of the necessity or propriety of any annexation at all upon that island-continent."

II

BISMARCK OPENS THE NEGOTIATIONS

BISMARCK'S adoption of a colonial policy in 1884 came as a complete surprise to the British Government. The German Chancellor had on many occasions refused to acquire colonies, had steadfastly opposed the popular demand for them in Germany, and had frequently expressed his opposition to colonization in the most definite terms. In fact he was never to the end of his days a real colonial enthusiast, and his adoption of a colonial policy was at best half-hearted. Nor are his motives for this departure entirely clear. He was perhaps somewhat affected by the economic changes in Germany during the 'seventies, and by the fact that certain of his former arguments against colonies no longer held good, but he was not a theorist, on the colonial question or any other question, and he was in general not greatly influenced by economic considerations. We can, of course, never know exactly what went on in his mind, but, so far as it is possible to judge, Bismarck appears to have inaugurated a colonial program largely for reasons of domestic policy, in the hope of pleasing German public opinion, stimulating national sentiment and securing by this means a working majority in the insubordinate Reichstag.

As early as 1868 Bismarck's attention was turned to colonial matters, and in that year he wrote to Roon a detailed exposition of his views on the subject. He contended that the promotion of colonies was a matter for private enterprise, and not for the government; he agreed with Roon that the navy was not strong enough to enable Germany to assume responsibilities overseas; he questioned the material advantage of colonies, held that they would be a cause of serious deficits, and thought it "difficult to justify the imposition of heavy taxation upon the whole nation for the benefit of a few branches of trade and industry"; and he feared that the establishment of colonies might lead to disputes with other nations.*

In the first ten years of the German Empire, Bismarck had a great number of practical opportunities as well as invitations from private individuals to annex territory overseas, and in every case without exception he refused to do so. In 1871, during the preliminary negotiations of the Treaty of Frankfort, he refused a French offer of colonies in Cochin China.† When, in 1872, the ruler of the Fiji Islands asked for the protection of the German Empire, Bismarck declined to give it.‡ In 1873 he told Lord Odo Russell that he desired neither colonies nor fleets: "Colonies, in his opinion, would only be a cause of weakness, because colonies could only be defended by powerful fleets, and Germany's geographical position did not necessitate her development into a first-class maritime power."§ In 1874 the Sultan of Zanzibar asked for the protection of the Empire, and Bismarck refused this request also, on the ground that he could not hope for support in the Reichstag.|| This excuse, that German public opinion would not support colonial ventures, was very frequently put forward by Bismarck during the 'seventies and early 'eighties. When, in 1876, a group of merchants (led by Weber and Lüderitz) brought forward a project for a German colony and protectorate in the Transvaal, Bismarck replied that he had come to the conclusion that "so great a nation as Germany could not, in the end, dispense with colonies; but, much as he was in principle in favor of the acquisition of colonies, the question was, however, so very difficult a one that he hesitated to undertake the matter without adequate

* 9 January 1868. Bismarck to Roon. W. H. Dawson: *The German Empire,* II, 174.

† M. E. Townsend: *The Rise and Fall of Germany's Colonial Empire,* p. 61.

‡ W. H. Dawson: *The German Empire,* II, 175.

§ 11 February 1873. Lord Odo Russell to Lord Granville. Lord Edmond Fitzmaurice: *Life of Lord Granville,* II, 337.

|| Max von Koschitzky: *Deutsche Colonialgeschichte,* I, 127.

preparation and a definite impulse from the nation itself." The situation, both foreign and domestic, was, he said, unfavorable. He added that a colonial project would have to be supported by a deep-seated national movement, of which there was so far no indication.* For the next few years Bismarck continued to oppose German colonization as much as ever, and in 1880 Prince Hohenlohe wrote of him: "Now, as before, he will not hear of colonies. He says we have not an adequate fleet to protect them, and our bureaucracy is not skilful enough to administer them."† And in 1881 Bismarck declared, in answer to a question of Count Frankenberg's: "So long as I am Chancellor we will carry on no colonial policy."‡

Even after he had adopted a colonial program, Bismarck's interest in colonies appears to have been only lukewarm, and frequently, during the negotiations with England, he insisted that he was being driven by public opinion to take a course which otherwise he might not have taken. He told the British Ambassador in Berlin, in October 1884, that "the colonial question in Germany had taken a hold on the sentiment of the German People, greater than that to which it was entitled, but that for the moment there was no restraining it."§ Two years later, when the German demand for colonies had been partially satisfied, he was ready enough to make friends with England, even at the cost of limiting his colonial demands. "This fault of our colonial Jingoes," he then wrote, "whose greed is greater than either we need or can satisfy, must be avoided with care."‖ Bismarck's policy was, in fact, primarily a European one. It was his object to balance the various and complicated factors in the European situation so

* Hahn and Wippermann: *Fürst Bismarck, Sein Politisches Leben und Wirken,* V, 3-4.

† 22 February 1880. W. H. Dawson: *The German Empire,* II, 176.

‡ H. von Poschinger: *Fürst Bismarck und die Parlamentarier,* III, 54.

§ 23 October 1884. Sir Edward Malet to Lord Granville, No. 331. Confidential. F.O. 64/1145.

‖ Marginal comment by Bismarck on despatch from Count Hatzfeldt to Bismarck, 19 October 1886. E. T. S. Dugdale: *German Diplomatic Documents, 1871-1914,* I, 227.

as to obtain security and peace for Germany, and this object was of far greater importance to him than any colonial acquisition. He astonished the explorer, Eugen Wolf, in December 1888 by saying: "Your map of Africa is very fine, but my map of Africa lies in Europe. Here lies Russia, and here" —pointing to the left—"lies France, and we are in the middle; that is my map of Africa."* Eckardstein declares that Bismarck's real feeling is shown by the remark which he made repeatedly in private circles: "The friendship of Lord Salisbury is worth more to me than twenty marshy colonies in Africa."†

But the situation in Germany changed rapidly during the early years of the empire, and many things occurred which might well have influenced Bismarck to change his views. Population was increasing at a tremendous rate, 2,507,000 during the years 1875-80, and 1,622,000 during the years 1880-85.‡ Emigration was also growing, from 46,371 in 1878 to 247,332 in 1881.§ The whole industrial system in Germany was stimulated and enlarged, not only by the necessity of absorbing the increase in population, but also, and very greatly, by Bismarck's conversion to protection in 1879. The enlargement of the industrial system in turn made necessary larger markets and larger supplies in raw materials. Thus, according to the economic theories at the basis of the imperialist movement, Germany's need for colonies was at this time greater than that of any other power. But there is no reason to assume that Bismarck accepted these theories, or that he was much influenced by economic considerations at all. He himself insisted that he did not begin to think along economic lines until he had been in office for fifteen years, and when reproached with disowning his earlier theories, as expressed in 1862, he replied: "I should be proud if I

* Bismarck: *Die Gesammelten Werke,* VIII, 646.

† Eckardstein: *Lebenserinnerungen und Politische Denkwürdigkeiten,* I, 307.

‡ W. H. Dawson: *The Evolution of Modern Germany,* p. 336.

§ *A History of the Peace Conference of Paris,* (edited by H. W. V. Temperley), II, 217.

could say that I held any economic theories at all in those days, but I must confess to my shame that I had none."* It might be said, even of his later life, that one of the chief defects of his political methods was that he did not entirely understand all the implications of the economic changes that were taking place in Europe, and failed to adapt himself to them.

But if economic forces could not greatly affect Bismarck, other forces could and did. During the 'seventies and 'eighties a tremendous popular movement in favor of colonies was growing up in Germany. This was stimulated by a number of different factors, one of which was undoubtedly the sudden burst of exploring activity in the middle and latter part of the nineteenth century. The achievement of German explorers in Africa in this period was magnificent. Under Böhm, Kaiser, and Reichard exploration was carried out in the direction of Lake Tanganyika and the upper waters of the Lualaba; Buchner, Pogge, and Wissmann worked in the region watered by the southern tributaries of the Congo; Schulze, Kund, and Wolff followed in the same direction; and in 1882-84 Flegel was active on the Niger and Benué.† Innumerable names could be cited in addition to these; Leichardt, Rebmann, Overweg, Barth, Krapf, Vogel, Beurmann, Peters, Maltzan, von der Decken, Rohlfs, Mauch, Nachtigal, Gustav and Clemens Denhardt, Güssfeld, Fritsch, Schweinfurth, Junker, Schnitzler, and many others.‡ Some of these explorers were not content to work for purely scientific purposes, but wanted Germany to gain direct advantages from the results of their labors. Von der Decken, who during the years 1860-65 explored the Kilimanjaro country and various parts of the East African coast, wrote home strongly urging the establishment of a colony in that region. Mauch expressed the hope that the Transvaal might become a German colony,

* W. H. Dawson: *The German Empire,* II, 10.
† J. S. Keltie: *The Partition of Africa,* p. 166.
‡ W. H. Dawson: *The German Empire,* II, 170-71.

and Rohlfs, returning to Germany after exploring the Cameroons, wrote: "Is it not deplorable that we are obliged to assist, inactive and without power to intervene, in the extension of England in Central Africa?"* A large part in the development of Africa was also taken by German missionaries. By 1884 the North German and the Basel Missionary Societies had some hundred stations all along the west coast of Africa, and other stations in the interior of Damaraland and Namaqualand, the two territories which were later combined to form German South West Africa.†

The appeals of German explorers met with a ready response from German economic writers and colonial propagandists. The foundations of modern colonial thought in Germany had been laid by Friedrich List, who proposed the acquisition of colonies as an outlet for emigration, and by Wilhelm Roscher, who urged that "Germany must lose no time if the last suitable territories are not to be seized by other and more resolute nations."‡ In 1879 Fabri brought out his *Bedarf Deutschland der Kolonieen,* emphasizing the need of colonies for emigration, and in 1881 Hübbe-Schleiden published his *Deutsche Kolonisation,* in which he insisted that the development of a self-conscious national feeling and of a strong oversea policy were questions of life and death for Germany's future.§ A further impetus was given to the movement by the foundation of a great number of colonial societies. The most important of these was the German Colonial Society, founded at Frankfort in December 1882, with the objects of disseminating colonial propaganda and of forming a central organization for the hitherto scattered efforts in the direction of colonial expansion. The Society gained over three thousand members by the end of its first year, and became strong enough to found an official organ,

* W. H. Dawson: *The German Empire,* II, 172-73.

† J. S. Keltie: *The Partition of Africa,* p. 170.

‡ W. H. Dawson: *The German Empire,* II, 171.

§ M. E. Townsend: *The Rise and Fall of Germany's Colonial Empire,* pp. 78-80.

the *Kolonialzeitung,* which appeared in January 1884. By the end of 1885 the Society had more than ten thousand members.*

Commercial circles also contributed their share to the colonial movement. German trade had established a foothold in Africa about the middle of the nineteenth century. The Woermanns and O'Swalds of Hamburg led the way, but they were followed by many other firms both of Hamburg and Bremen, and by the beginning of 1884 there were some fifteen German firms which had among them about sixty factories on the west coast of Africa.† Hamburg and Bremen came into especial prominence during the 'eighties because of their entry, after a considerable struggle in the case of Hamburg, into the German Customs Union. By a law of 16 February 1882 Hamburg agreed to become a member of the union on 1 October 1888, and the incorporation of Bremen was effected by a law of 31 March 1885.‡ Both cities were heavily interested in Africa, and the trade they carried on there was hampered by the tariffs imposed by the Cape, which had recently been applied to Walfisch Bay as well.§ The annexation by England of the Fiji Islands in 1874 caused irritation in commercial circles, and this was increased when England set aside as invalid the land claims of a number of German settlers there. Bismarck took up these claims, and pressed them vigorously, until they were submitted to arbitration by a mixed commission in 1885. When, in April 1883, Bismarck addressed a formal inquiry to the senates of the three Hanseatic cities, asking them to express their views as to what would be the most effective means to protect and encourage German trade,|| the senates of Hamburg and Bremen sent replies pointing in the direction of colonial annexations. Hamburg, in particular, asked for the protection

* M. E. Townsend: *The Rise and Fall of Germany's Colonial Empire,* pp. 82–83.

† J. S. Keltie: *The Partition of Africa,* p. 170.

‡ W. H. Dawson: *The German Empire,* II, 29.

§ J. S. Keltie: *The Partition of Africa,* p. 174.

|| 14 April 1883. Instructions to the German Minister in Hamburg. German White Book, *Togogebiet und Biafra-Bai,* No. 1.

of Germans in unannexed territories by treaties and by the stationing of warships along the coast, the foundation of a naval station at Fernando Po, and the acquisition of the coast of Biafra Bay.*

Bismarck was genuinely concerned about the protection of German trade, and even before 1870 he gave, as chancellor of Prussia, very considerable assistance to certain commercial houses in the South Seas.† In 1874 he wrote: "If the Government of his Majesty renounces the pursuance of a colonial policy of its own, it is all the more bound to protect German trade against unjustifiable interferences."‡ In 1876 and 1879 he negotiated treaties giving Germany commercial rights in the Tongan Islands and Samoa.§ It cannot be doubted that the desire to protect German trade played an important part in Bismarck's decision to adopt a colonial policy. Herbert Bismarck told Lord Granville in June 1884 that "we wished neither now nor later for Colonies in the English sense, but only immediate protection for our countrymen." Granville replied that Germany would come to colonies all the same, on which Prince Bismarck commented, when he saw a report of the conversation: "Possibly; but we do not wish to create them artificially. If they arise we shall do our best to protect them."|| About the same time he also wrote: "What is a Colonial policy? We must protect our countrymen."¶

But the influence upon Bismarck which seems to have been greatest is that of public opinion. Again and again, in his conversations and in his despatches, there appear references to this factor. He told Sir Philip Currie in September 1885 that he had never favored the colonial idea himself but that

* 6 July 1883. Report of the Chamber of Commerce in Hamburg. German White Book, *Togogebiet und Biafra-Bai,* No. 3.

† Charles Lowe: *Prince Bismarck,* II, 211-12.

‡ 4 March 1874. W. H. Dawson: *The German Empire,* II, 176.

§ M. E. Townsend: *The Rise and Fall of Germany's Colonial Empire,* p. 70.

|| 16 June 1884. Count Herbert Bismarck to Prince Bismarck. E. T. S. Dugdale: *German Diplomatic Documents, 1871-1914,* I, 179.

¶ Marginal comment by Bismarck on a despatch from Münster to Bismarck of 7 June 1884. E. T. S. Dugdale: *German Diplomatic Documents, 1871-1914,* I, 178.

"he could not refrain from turning the Colonial stream into the main channel of his Parliamentary policy."* He said to Lord Ampthill, in regard to Angra Pequena, that he feared that "deep and lasting disappointment will be felt by Public Opinion in Germany if H.M.G. cannot suggest a satisfactory settlement of the question."† Lord Ampthill considered the whole colonial controversy to be a gigantic electioneering maneuver on the part of Bismarck, who, he wrote, "is taking advantage of the national craze that England opposes Germany's Colonial Aspirations, as an election cry, which may finally secure him the working majority in the coming elections, he had bid for in vain in the two former general elections to the Reichstag."‡ Ampthill's theory is supported by Bismarck's own statements. He wrote to Münster in January 1885 that "the Colonial question is already a matter of life and death for reasons of domestic policy. . . . Public opinion in Germany lays so great a stress on our Colonial Policy, that the Government's position in the country actually depends on its success. . . . The smallest corner of New Guinea or West Africa, even if quite worthless in itself, is just now of greater import to our policy than the whole of Egypt and its future. . . ."§ This is of a piece with Bismarck's other statement, which has already been quoted, that Lord Salisbury's friendship was worth more than twenty colonies in Africa. For Bismarck, colonies were a means and not an end.

It is important to note that a colonial policy was one of the few devices by which national feeling in the Reichstag could be organized, for it was almost the only question of this kind on which the Reichstag was entitled to vote. The normal quota of numbers for the army and the requisite financial

* Summary of Memorandum by Sir Philip Currie of his conversations with Prince Bismarck, 28-30 September 1885. Lady Gwendolen Cecil: *Life of Lord Salisbury*, III, 257.

† 14 June 1884. Lord Ampthill to Lord Granville. Private. Granville Private MSS, G.D. 29/178.

‡ 16 August 1884. Lord Ampthill to Lord Granville. Private. Granville Private MSS, G.D. 29/178.

§ 25 January 1885. Prince Bismarck to Count Münster. E. T. S. Dugdale: *German Diplomatic Documents, 1871-1914*, I, 189.

means were actually part of the imperial constitution (Articles 60-68). It was only when additions were required that the Reichstag was consulted. On the other hand, the navy and the colonies were not provided for under the constitution. Hence the Reichstag had entire control of the appropriations for these purposes.

Bismarck's shift to a colonial policy was not due to a single factor but to a whole complexity of motives. The popular movement for colonies, the explorers, the missionaries, the colonial societies, pressure from commercial interests that were becoming increasingly prominent; all these played a part. Bearing more indirectly on his action were the growth of the German mercantile marine and the plans for construction of the Kaiser Wilhelm (Kiel) Canal under discussion in 1883-84, which was of the first importance for shipping and which designated Germany more definitely as a mercantile nation. Finally, the international situation in 1883 and 1884 was exceptionally favorable for Germany: Bismarck's position on the continent was rendered secure by the Triple Alliance and the League of the Three Emperors. England and France, moreover, having quarreled over Egypt, were not prepared to act jointly in opposition to what Bismarck might wish to do, while separately neither one was strong enough to gainsay him.

In November 1882, F. A. E. Lüderitz, a merchant of Bremen who had long been active in the South African trade, and who was one of the leaders of the group which proposed a German colony in the Transvaal to Bismarck in 1876, wrote to the German foreign office that he was about to send a ship with assorted cargo to a place on the southwest coast of Africa which was still in the possession of native rulers. He was giving his supercargo full powers to make contracts with the natives securing the monopoly of trade and the possession of land for factories and plantations. In order not to be disturbed in his possession, he desired "to place it under the protection of the flag of the German Empire immediately upon the conclusion of the contracts." He asked whether, and under what conditions, this protection could be granted to him, and offered to give testimonials as to his financial standing, and to call at the foreign office to give further information about his project.* Lüderitz was ascertained to be a merchant of good reputation, and in January 1883 he was allowed to call at the German foreign office, in order to state his demands more clearly. These demands were, for the most part, restricted to the request "for that general protection which the empire regularly allows to extend to the interests of Germans living abroad." Lüderitz asked that the territories in which he proposed to establish himself might be placed within the jurisdiction (*Amtsbezirk*) of the nearest imperial consul, and that a German warship might occasionally visit the coast (1). Such a request was by no means a new thing, for Bismarck had often before given consular protection to German traders in unoccupied territories, and Lüderitz was, accordingly, confidentially informed that Bismarck had expressed himself in agreement with his demands, but that certain information must be obtained from London before a final answer could be given.†

A despatch was now addressed, on 4 February 1883, to the German chargé d'affaires in London, Count Herbert Bismarck, describing Lüderitz's undertaking and his request for German protection, and stating that, although there was no objection to granting him this protection, Bismarck wanted the British Government to be informed of these plans, in case that they "should now perhaps exercise rights of sovereignty in those regions or intend to grant protection." But the German Government reserved the right to grant the protection itself if the settlements in question lay outside the English influence or the influence of another friendly power. Such was the despatch as it appeared later in the German White Book on Angra Pequena, which was laid before the Reichstag on 11 December 1884. But two very important

* 16 November 1882. F. A. E. Lüderitz to the German foreign office. German White Book, *Angra Pequena,* No. 1. Full version in Reichsarchiv, Vermischtes Südwestafrika I.

† 20 January 1883. Holleben to Lüderitz. Copy. Reichsarchiv, Vermischtes Südwestafrika I.

passages were left out of the published version. It was made clear, in the original despatch, that if the German Government granted protection to Lüderitz, it would be merely "in the manner and in the degree in which the empire generally allows it [protection] to extend to the interests of its citizens living abroad." Count Herbert Bismarck was also asked to say that "now, as formerly, we have no thought of any oversea projects, and especially of any interference in existing British interests in South Africa, so that we would only be pleased if England eventually wished to permit her effectual protection to extend to German settlers in those regions" (2). There is no reason to believe that this despatch did not represent Bismarck's intentions at the time it was sent. Lüderitz had requested only that protection which Bismarck had been giving to German traders for many years past, assistance from the nearest German consul and an occasional visit from a German warship. There is no evidence that Bismarck had decided upon a colonial policy by February 1883. He was willing to grant Lüderitz the protection required, but he had no objection to allowing this protection to be given by the British Government, if the acquisitions of Lüderitz lay within the British influence. The effect of the despatch was, however, very misleading. It created the impression that the German Government was opposed to a colonial policy, and this impression remained, since the despatch was never contradicted. Both Count Münster, the German ambassador in London, and Lord Granville were completely deceived as to Bismarck's intentions, and as late as 6 June 1884 Münster quoted the despatch of 4 February 1883 as evidence that his personal attitude of opposition to German colonial attempts was in agreement with Bismarck's policy.* Count Herbert Bismarck later admitted to Lord Granville "that the views of the German Government had not perhaps been quite so clearly stated as might have been done."† Bismarck can, per-

* 6 June 1884. Münster to Bismarck. Reichsarchiv, Vermischtes Südwestafrika III.

† 14 June 1884. Lord Granville to Lord Ampthill. No. 169A. Draft. F.O. 64/1102. This passage was omitted when this despatch was later published in the British Blue Book, (C. 4190), No. 69, Enclosure.

haps, be justly criticized for not making the situation clear when he at length decided upon a colonial policy, and the fact that the two passages quoted above were omitted from the White Book indicates that he felt he had done something which was difficult to defend or to explain.

The original wording of the despatch of 4 February 1883 also throws light on another matter. Scholars have found it difficult to explain why Bismarck, when he knew from previous correspondence and from British state papers presented to Parliament that England had no title to the mainland at Angra Pequena, thought it necessary to inquire about her claims once again before proceeding to take the place himself. It now appears that at the time of his first inquiry Bismarck probably did not desire colonies at all. He had no objection to letting England furnish protection to Lüderitz if she could do so. In fact, the whole tone of the despatch, "we would only be pleased if England, etc.," makes it clear that Bismarck was quite ready to accept British protection for Lüderitz if it were practically possible, and that he addressed his inquiry to England with this possibility in mind. It is true that Bismarck reserved the right to grant protection if Lüderitz's settlement lay outside the English influence, but "influence" is a broad and inclusive term, and it is striking, in view of subsequent developments, that he did not use a more restrictive expression such as "jurisdiction" or "possession." It was not until later, when Bismarck finally decided on a colonial policy, that he began to inquire narrowly about England's title. The change in his terminology when he brought the subject up again in September clearly reflects his change in attitude.

The instructions of 4 February 1883 were accurately carried out by Count Herbert Bismarck in London. Sir Julian Pauncefote reported him as saying that if England could not protect the settlement of Lüderitz, the German Government would "do their best to extend to it the same measure of protection which they give to their subjects in remote parts of the world, but without having the least design to establish any footing in South Africa."* Münster reported to Berlin that Pauncefote's attention had been especially called to the fact "that we would only be pleased if England were in the position to allow her protection to extend to German settlements in those regions" (3). This last passage was also omitted from the German White Book, though the rest of Münster's despatch was published.

Sir Julian Pauncefote privately communicated the German inquiry to Sir Robert Herbert of the colonial office,† and in accordance with Herbert's suggestions a reply to the German ambassador was drafted, sent to the colonial office for concurrence,‡ and finally signed by Lord Granville on 23 February 1883. This reply stated that the Cape Colony had certain establishments along the coast, but that, "without more precise information as to the spot where the German factory will be established, it is not possible to form any opinion as to whether the British authorities would have it in their power to give it any protection in case of need.

"If however the German Government would be good enough to furnish the required information, it would be forwarded to the Government of the Cape Colony with instructions to report whether and to what extent their wishes could be met."§ Münster sent this answer back to Berlin three days later, but Bismarck made no reply to the British question and took no further diplomatic action in the matter until the following September.

Bismarck asserted later that he was prevented by illness from following the matter up.|| His attention was called to the question again when Lüderitz put in an appearance at

* 7 February 1883. Minute by Sir Julian Pauncefote of a Conversation with Count Herbert Bismarck. British Blue Book, (C. 4265), Appendix IV, No. 1, Enclosure 1.

† 12 February 1883. Minute by Sir Julian Pauncefote, F.O. 64/1101.

‡ 15 February 1883. Foreign office to colonial office. British Blue Book, (C. 4265), Appendix IV, No. 1.

§ 23 February 1883. Granville to Münster. British Blue Book, (C. 4265), Appendix IV, No. 1, Enclosure 2.

|| 10 June 1884. Bismarck to Münster. German White Book, *Angra Pequena*, No. 24.

the German foreign office in August 1883, and inquired whether the German Government would recognize the rights which he claimed and was prepared to protect him in the possession of a trading post he had established at the small harbor of Angra Pequena. Von Bojanowski, the representative of the foreign office who talked with him, replied that, as Lüderitz had been informed already, he could as a citizen of the empire reckon with certainty upon that protection which the empire was generally able to give to its citizens. Von Bojanowski gathered that Lüderitz had only made a private purchase, and concluded that such a purchase could not transfer the rights of sovereignty, so that if Lüderitz perhaps thought the land acquired by him should be looked upon as belonging to Germany, such a view of the matter could not be opposed too vigorously. As far as protection from unfriendly natives was concerned, von Bojanowski thought Lüderitz should take care of that himself, but the admiralty would certainly be willing to send a ship there from time to time, if it was a question of punishing unfriendly tribes. Herr Lüderitz expressed the conviction that no danger from the natives was to be apprehended, but feared ill will and attacks upon his rights and undertakings from the side of the English. He said it was clear that Spence (an English trader with an establishment at Angra Pequena) was making difficulties for him, and he hoped to get the English out of their position there. He desired that his undertaking might be recommended to the protection of the imperial German consul in Cape Town.

In commenting on von Bojanowski's report, Bismarck made clear his own opinion that even if Lüderitz had purchased the rights of sovereignty, "such rights would be transferred not to the empire but to Lüderitz, as sovereign of Angra Pequena." If England had not taken possession, the sovereignty remained "either with the negro chief in question or with Lüderitz; not with the empire." Concerning the protection of Lüderitz, Bismarck wrote: "We will always try to protect his justly acquired rights so long as he is a

German subject," and he agreed that the admiralty might send a ship to Angra Pequena from time to time. Bismarck commented on Lüderitz's fear of attacks: "Recommend the London Embassy to make discreet inquiry. That England, with the German tendency of a part of the Dutch farmers, will not look upon a German establishment four days' journey from Cape Town with pleasure, is to be assumed." He agreed to Lüderitz's request for a recommendation to the Cape Consul, but insisted that he must give up the idea of pushing the English out, and rather seek good relations with the English authorities (4).

Bismarck's comments indicate that his attitude in regard to this undertaking had changed. His admission that the activities of Lüderitz will probably be displeasing to England, and his wish for secrecy which is expressed in the phrase "discreet inquiry," indicate that, while he had not yet perhaps determined on a colonial policy, he was taking a special and unusual interest in the Lüderitz development, and was considering further steps.

This hint is corroborated by the instructions which Bismarck gave on 15 August 1883 for a press notice on the subject of Angra Pequena. He wished it to be emphasized that the Bremen firm "could count on the protection of the German Government so far as its undertaking did not conflict with the rights of others, and that it should also be pointed out how the government could not go further, after the experience it had had with the rejection of the Samoa Bill, where German interests very much further developed had been concerned. By the treatment of the Samoa question on the part of the people's representatives . . . the government was discouraged, and did not believe it could reckon upon sympathy in the Reichstag for an oversea policy" (5). This looks very much as if Bismarck was testing German public opinion, to find out how it would react to a more vigorous colonial policy.

Instructions were sent to Lippert, the German consul at Cape Town, on 18 August 1883, informing him that Bismarck had granted Lüderitz's request for protection, so far as his claims did not conflict with the claims of others, and asking him to help Lüderitz with his advice as well as to give him consular protection. It was added (in a passage omitted from the German White Book) that Lüderitz should seek good relations with the English authorities, that he should be recommended to maintain especial reserve in the use of the English and German press, and that he should be advised not to discuss in the future the attitude of the German Government towards his projects (6). Again the emphasis on secrecy will be observed.

The negotiations with London were reopened when, on 10 September 1883, Baron von Plessen, the German chargé d'affaires, called at the British foreign office to leave a *Promemoria,* in which it was asked whether Her Majesty's Government claimed the suzerainty over Angra Pequena, and, if so, on what grounds they based their claim. In leaving the *Promemoria,* Plessen explained that he was instructed to ask only for the private information of his government. In the same unofficial manner he also inquired what view the British Government would take of the proceedings of Lüderitz, and whether they had any objection to them.

The British foreign office immediately wrote to the colonial office, informing them of the German communication, and adding: "I am to request that you will move the Earl of Derby to inform Lord Granville what answer should be returned to these inquiries."* On 2 October the colonial office replied that a British subject, Daniel De Pass, claimed to have prior rights of purchase over the territory stated to have been acquired by Lüderitz. They added that the islands adjacent to Angra Pequena had been annexed to the Cape Colony in 1867, "but that Her Majesty's Government have no claims or jurisdiction over the mainland."† On the basis

* 22 September 1883. Foreign office to colonial office. British Blue Book, (C. 4190), No. 15. The passage quoted is omitted from the Blue Book. Full version in F.O. 64/1101.

† 2 October 1883. Colonial office to foreign office. British Blue Book, (C. 4190), No. 16. The words quoted are omitted from the Blue Book. Full version in F.O. 64/1101.

of this letter, the foreign office drafted a note to Count Münster and a memorandum to accompany it, giving the information they had received from the colonial office, and stating that the British Government had no claims or jurisdiction over the mainland.* But before these documents were sent off, the colonial office wrote again, this time privately, saying that "Mr. Scanlen, the Cape Premier, has raised some questions concerning the place, and if by any chance you have not told the German Embassy that this country 'has no claims or jurisdiction over the mainland' please do not do so at present."† The foreign office had in fact not yet replied to Münster, and the note to him which had been drafted was now suspended.

Mr. Scanlen, the Prime Minister of the Cape Colony, was at this time in England, where he remained until January 1884. He was very much disturbed by the German activities at Angra Pequena, and appears to have exerted his influence to the utmost to induce the British Government to take some step in the matter. Writing to a member of his cabinet in Cape Town, he described "the course I have been urging upon Sir R. Herbert, and public men with whom I came into contact, that England should at the very least go the length of saying that between Cape Frio on the west and Delagoa Bay on the east there should be a South African Monroe Doctrine, and all European powers be given to understand that it must be 'hands off.' Sir R. Herbert, the first time I spoke to him, coincided in this view. . . ."‡

The fact that Mr. Scanlen interfered at this point, and was successful in representing the colonial point of view, is of the greatest importance for the negotiations that followed. For, had the foreign office replied to Münster as the colonial office at first suggested (and this would have happened if the foreign office had not waited for thirty-six days before taking action) there would quite possibly have been no fric-

* October 1883. Draft of note to Count Münster, suspended. F.O. 64/1101.

† 7 November 1883. Sir Robert G. W. Herbert to Sir Philip Currie. Private. F.O. 64/1101.

‡ 29 November 1883. T. Scanlen to J. X. Merriman. Sir Perceval Laurence: *Life of John Xavier Merriman,* p. 85.

tion between England and Germany in regard to Angra Pequena. Bismarck would have had the official statement which he tried so hard to obtain, that England had no claims on the mainland, and England, in view of such a statement, could hardly have objected to the German occupation.

Meanwhile Bismarck was becoming impatient at not receiving an answer, and on 16 November 1883, Count Münster called again at the foreign office and repeated his questions verbally, but now officially.* The colonial office, again pressed for a reply, wrote to the foreign office on 21 November 1883, suggesting the terms of an answer to Count Münster (7). A note in these terms was drawn up in the foreign office, signed by Granville, and despatched to Münster the same day. It stated that "although Her Majesty's Government have not proclaimed the Queen's sovereignty along the whole country, but only at certain points, such as Walfisch Bay and the Angra Pequena Islands, they consider that any claim to sovereignty or jurisdiction by a Foreign Power between the southern point of Portuguese jurisdiction at latitude 18 and the frontier of the Cape Colony would infringe their legitimate rights."†

Such a claim was preposterous. It represented a complete triumph for Mr. Scanlen and his theory of a Monroe Doctrine for South Africa. Lord Derby, who was always easily bullied by the colonists, had permitted him to have his own way entirely. And not only was Scanlen's influence great with the colonial office, but, in regard to Angra Pequena, the colonial office now ruled the foreign office. On 24 November, Granville's note to Münster of 21 November was sent to the colonial office, and the covering letter ended: "I am to add that Lord Granville concurs generally in the course which Lord Derby proposes to pursue with regard to this question."‡

* 12 November 1883. Instructions to Count Herbert Bismarck in London. German White Book, *Angra Pequena,* No. 5. 17 November 1883. British foreign office to colonial office. British Blue Book, (C. 4190), No. 29.

† 21 November 1883. Granville to Münster. British Blue Book, (C. 4190), No. 30.

‡ 24 November 1883. Foreign office to colonial office. Draft. F.O. 64/1101.

Not only was the British claim unreasonable, but the German inquiries had not even been answered. Although the British Government had put forward a general claim to exclude other countries from South West Africa, they had made no statement as to whether or not they claimed the suzerainty of that region, and they had certainly not shown any title on which a claim to the suzerainty could be based.

At this stage in the negotiations Lüderitz reported to Bismarck, on 20 November 1883, that his representative had purchased for him all the rest of the coast of South West Africa, from the Orange River northwards to 26 degrees of south latitude.* The undertaking had now assumed large proportions, and this fact no doubt acted as an additional stimulus to the German foreign office.

Upon Bismarck's command, a note was now drafted and on 27 December 1883 was sent to Münster to be delivered by him to the British foreign office.† The subject of Angra Pequena was discussed thoroughly, and the claims of the British Government and their former utterances on the subject were described in detail. It was pointed out that in state papers laid before Parliament the British Government had expressly declared that the territory in question was not under the Queen's sovereignty. It was then stated that, if the British Government should claim the wide territory between the Orange River and 18 degrees of south latitude, which had hitherto passed for independent, the German Government would esteem it of importance to know upon what title this claim was grounded, and what arrangements England had there to grant this protection to German subjects, so as to relieve Germany from granting it herself.‡ This note was handed in by Count Münster on 31 December 1883. It remained unanswered for six and a half months.

* 20 November 1883. Lüderitz to Bismarck. German White Book, *Angra Pequena,* No. 6.

† 27 December 1883. Instructions to Count Münster. German White Book, *Angra Pequena,* No. 8.

‡ 31 December 1883. Münster to British foreign office. German White Book, *Angra Pequena,* No. 9.

NOTES

1. 17 January 1883. *Promemoria* by Count Hatzfeldt. Reichsarchiv, Vermischtes Südwestafrika I.

"Der Kaufmann F.A.E. Lüderitz in Bremen . . . hat vor Kurzem sich hier persönlich vorgestellt, um seine bezüglichen Wünsche näher zu präcisiren.

"Dieselbe erscheinen, im Gegensatz zu den in früheren Eingaben des Genannten enthaltenen, wesentlich herabgestimmt und beschränken sich in der Hauptsache auf die Bitte um denjenigen allgemeinen Schutz, wie ihn das Reich den Interessen der im Auslande lebenden Deutschen regelmässig angedeihen lässt.

". . . Er bittet nun speziell, die respektiven Gebiete, in denen er sich etabliren wird, dem Amtsbezirk des nächsten Kaiserlichen Konsulats (wahrscheinlich würde dies das Konsulat in Capstadt sein) (Bismarck: ja) zuzutheilen, ferner würde es ihm erwünscht sein, wenn in den Küstengewässern dort, wo seine Besitzungen belegen sind, ein Kaiserliches Kriegsschiff gelegentlich die Flagge zeigte. . . ."

2. 4 February 1883. Instructions to Count Herbert Bismarck, the German chargé d'affaires in London. German White Book, *Angra Pequena,* No. 2. Full version in draft in Reichsarchiv, Vermischtes Südwestafrika I. The two passages quoted in the text are as follows, the words deleted from the version published in the White Book being indicated by italics:

"Obwohl an sich nichts im Wege steht, dem betreffenden Unternehmen diesen Schutz *in der Art und in dem Masse* zu gewähren, *in welchem das Reich ihn den Interessen seiner im Auslande lebenden Angehöriger überhaupt angedeihen lässt,* so ist es mir doch erwünscht, die grossbritannische Regierung von diesen Plänen für den Fall unterrichtet zu wissen, dass dieselbe jetzt etwa in jenen Gegenden Souveränitätsrechte ausüben oder Schutz zu gewähren beabsichtigen sollte."

"Eventuell stelle ich anheim, *dabei* zu sagen, *dass uns jetzt wie früher alle überseeischen Projekte und insbesondere jede Einmischung in vorhandene britische Interessen in Süd-Afrika fern lägen, sowie dass wir es nur gern sehen würden, wenn eventuell England deutschen Ansiedlern in jenen Gegenden seinen wirksamen Schutz angedeihen lassen wollte,* das wir *aber* selbstverständlich uns vorbehalten, diesen Schutz unsererseits dann eintreten zu lassen, wenn die betreffenden Ansiedlungen ausserhalb des englischen Einflusses oder des Einflusses einer anderen befreundeten Macht lägen."

A part of the second of these two passages has been quoted in Paul Darmstaedter: *Geschichte der Aufteilung und Kolonisation Afrikas,* II, 60-61.

3. 26 February 1883. Münster to Bismarck, reporting on the execution of the instructions of 4 February. German White Book, *Angra Pequena,* No. 4. Full version in Reichsarchiv, Vermischtes Südwestafrika I. The following passage is omitted from the version published in the White Book:

"Es war dabei im Sinne des Erlasses Sir J. Pauncefote gegenüber besonders hervorgehoben, dass wir es nur gern sehen würden, wenn England in der Lage wäre, deutschen Ansiedlungen in jenen Gegenden seinen Schutz angedeihen zu lassen."

4. 8 August 1883. Memorandum by von Bojanowski on two conversations with Lüderitz. Reichsarchiv, Vermischtes Südwestafrika I. The passages on which Bismarck made marginal comments are as follows:

"Nach seiner (des Herrn Lüderitz) Darstellung sandte es sich im vorliegenden Falle lediglich um ein Privatgeschäft (Kauf); ein solches Privatgeschäft vermöge nicht Souveränitätsrechte zu übertragen, (Bismarck: ? auch wenn dass geschähe, so wären solche Rechte nicht auf das Reich, sondern auf Lüderitz, als Souverän von Angra P. übergegangen.) und könne daher, wenn Herr Lüderitz etwa meine, dass das von ihm erworbene Land fortab als zum deutschen Reiche gehörig angesehen werden solle, einer derartigen Unterstellung nicht bestimmt genug entgegentreten werden. Dei Frage über die Souveränität über das ihm (dem p. Lüderitz) abgetretene Land und in Betreff der Besitz- und Eigenthumsverhältnisse an jenen drei Inseln würden sorgfältig zu prüfen sein. . . . (Bismarck: namentlich die etwaigen Ansprüche Englands; hat dieses nicht Besitz erworben oder ergriffen, so steht die Landeshoheit entweder bei dem betreffenden Negerfürsten oder bei Lüderitz; nicht beim Reich.)

"Wenn es ihm darauf ankomme etwa die Geschäftsangestellten und die Faktoreien gegen Belästigungen durch feindliche Hottentottenstämme gesichert zu sehen, so werde ihm nur Selbsthilfe anzurathen sein. (Bismarck: ? seine rite erworbene Rechte werden wir immer zu schützen suchen, so lange er Deutscher Unterthan ist.)"

"So sei bereits jetzt unverkennbar, dass Herr Spence ihm Schwierigkeiten mache (Bismarck: London B. vorsichtige Erkundigung empfehlen. Dass England bei der deutschen Tendenz eines Theils der holländischen Bauern ein deutsches Etablissement 4 Tagereisen von Kapstadt nicht gern sieht, ist anzunehmen.) . . ."

". . . er trachtet dahin die Engländer aus ihrer dortigen Position, die übrigens wenig bieten soll, zu vertreiben. (Bismarck: das muss er sich vergehn lassen, vielmehr gute Beziehungen zu engl. Behörden suchen.)"

5. 15 August 1883. Count Herbert Bismarck in Kissingen to Count Hatzfeldt. Reichsarchiv, Vermischtes Südwestafrika I.

". . . Seine Durchlaucht ist mit einer Erwähnung des Gegenstandes in der Presse einverstanden, wünscht aber, dass dabei mehr, als dem p. Lüderitz gegenüber geschehen, accentuirt werde, dass die Bremer Firma auf den Schutz der Deutschen Regierung rechnen könne, so weit ihr Unternehmen nicht mit fremden Rechten collidiren würde, und dass ferner hervorgehoben werde, wie die Regierung nicht weitergehen könne, nach der Erfahrung die sie bei Ablehnung der Vorlage wegen Samoa gemacht hätte, wo es sich um sehr viel weiter entwickelte Deutsche Interessen gehandelt hätte. Durch die Behandlung der Samoa-Frage seitens der Volksvertretung, . . . , sei die Regierung entmuthigt und glaube nicht für eine überseeische Politik auf Sympathien im Reichstage rechnen zu können."

6. 18 August 1883. Bismarck to Lippert. German White Book, *Angra Pequena,* No. 3. Full version in Draft in Reichsarchiv, Vermischtes Südwestafrika I. The following passage is omitted from the White Book:

"Desgleichen erscheint es nicht überflüssig, Herrn Lüderitz noch eine besondere Zurückhaltung in der Benutzung der englischen und deutschen Presse für sein Unternehmen zu empfehlen, und den Rath zu ertheilen, namentlich auch die angebliche Stellung der Kaiserlichen Regierung zu seinen Projekten künftig unerörtert zu lassen."

7. 21 November 1883. Colonial office to foreign office, immediate. F.O. 64/1101. The second paragraph begins as follows:

"2. Lord Derby is of opinion that the German Government should be informed, in answer to their inquiries on the subject: that it has always been understood that, although Her Majesty's Government have not proclaimed the Queen's Sovereignty along the whole country, but only at certain points, such as Walwich [sic] Bay and the Angra Pequena Islands, no foreign sovereignty or jurisdiction is admissible between the southern point of Portuguese jurisdiction at latitude 18 and the frontier of the Cape Colony."

III

THE BRITISH RECEPTION OF BISMARCK'S INQUIRIES

COUNT MÜNSTER'S note of 31 December 1883 was sent to Lord Derby for his consideration on 19 January 1884.* The foreign office now left the matter entirely in the hands of the colonial office and took no further step until June 1884 except to inform the colonial office of the various German communications as they were made. There was some precedent for consultation between these two departments, and in 1880 Lord Granville had written a minute approving of it: "There is no reason why such friendly intercommunication should not continue. The dangers which Mr. Currie apprehends from the conflicting objects of the Foreign and Colonial Offices ought not to exist, and are not likely to prevail especially under the general superintendence of Lord Kimberley, who is so well acquainted with Foreign Affairs."† Lord Derby had served as foreign secretary and was also well acquainted with foreign affairs, and no doubt Granville felt he should be able to give his colleague considerable freedom for this reason. But there was a great difference between communicating judiciously with the colonial office, and allowing it to direct almost completely negotiations with a foreign power, which was what happened in this case. Lord Granville's more or less complete delegation of authority was prompted by a peculiar combination of circumstances.

Writing to Count Herbert Bismarck in October 1884, Granville gave his excuse for "having acted as it were, only as a medium of communication between the German Gov-

* 19 January 1884. Foreign office to colonial office. British Blue Book, (C. 4190), No. 38.

† 6 May 1880. Minute by Lord Granville. Private Granville MSS, G.D. 29/143.

ernment, and the Colonial Office on the Angra Pequena affair." He said: "From what I constantly had been told by Ampthill as his own opinion and as that of Count Hatzfeldt, I was convinced that Prince Bismarck far from taking an interest in these colonization schemes was strongly opposed to them, and for that reason there was no diplomatic reason for my stirring much in the matter."* He gave the same explanation to Dilke: "I had continually the most positive assurances in London, and still more in Berlin, that Bismarck was dead against German colonization, as he was."† There were certainly some grounds for this excuse. The instructions from Berlin of 4 February 1883, which have already been described, tended very strongly to create the impression that the German Government was not interested in colonies. Münster, as has been shown, did not realize until June 1884 that Bismarck desired a colonial policy, and his communications to the British foreign office can hardly have helped to make Bismarck's intentions clear. Nor did Granville receive much assistance from his representative in Berlin, Lord Ampthill. The tenor of Lord Ampthill's despatches had always been that Bismarck was strongly opposed to German colonization, and this is what he continued to report even so late as May 1884. The "assurances" he sent to Granville were not properly assurances at all, they were merely statements of his own opinion, and of what he had heard from Count Hatzfeldt, the German foreign secretary. Such statements could not bind the German Government in any way, but they gave the very definite impression that Bismarck was unalterably opposed to colonial ventures. In April 1883, Lord Ampthill was asked to report whether there was any foundation for the rumor which had come to the notice of the British minister at Brussels, that a company was about to be

* 2 October 1884. Lord Granville to Count Herbert Bismarck. Draft. Private. Private Granville MSS, G.D. 29/207.

† 24 September 1884. Lord Granville to Sir Charles W. Dilke. Gwynn and Tuckwell: *Life of Sir Charles W. Dilke,* II, 81-82. In the life of Dilke, the text is correct, but the date is wrongly given as 27 September. Cf. the draft of this letter and Dilke's reply of 25 September in Private Granville MSS, G.D. 29/122.

formed in Germany for the purpose of colonizing New Guinea.* Ampthill replied immediately that he had already called Count Hatzfeldt's attention to this at an evening party. Count Hatzfeldt "observed laughingly that Prince Bismarck, as I knew, had always and steadily resisted the national desire in Germany for the acquisition of colonies, but that when in the future the present Government was no more and the Party in favor of Colonies succeeded to Power in Germany, it appeared to him that England and France would have taken good care to leave them none to annex."† A few days later Ampthill wrote again in regard to the same subject and stated that he had asked the German foreign secretary "whether I was correct in reporting to Your Lordship that the above-named Company was a private one and not as yet supported by the Imperial German Government.—His Excellency replied that my impression was correct,—besides which the Imperial Government did not promote any scheme for the increase of emigration from Germany as I well knew."‡

Besides this, Lord Ampthill frequently gave expression to his own opinion as to the unlikelihood of colonial developments in Germany. The following passage will serve as an illustration. In March 1883, after describing the great desire for colonies in Germany, Ampthill wrote: "Prince Bismarck is opposed to the National wish, as I have often had occasion to state in my previous correspondence, and he will be able to keep down and prevent any serious agitation in Germany for the purchase and foundation of Colonies so long as he [is] Chancellor of the Empire."§ Statements of this kind were repeated again and again in Ampthill's dispatches (1), and even on 30 May 1884 he spoke of the growing impatience of

* 24 April 1883. Lord Granville to Lord Ampthill. Draft. No. 178. F.O. 64/1144.

† 27 April 1883. Lord Ampthill to Lord Granville. Draft. No. 142. Secret. F.O. 244/363.

‡ 3 May 1883. Lord Ampthill to Lord Granville. No. 149. Draft. F.O. 244/363.

§ 29 March 1883. Lord Ampthill to Lord Granville. No. 109. Draft. F.O. 244/363.

the German people for the inauguration of a colonial policy by Prince Bismarck, "who has hitherto shown no inclination to satisfy their desire for colonies beyond sending Doctor Nachtigal on board the 'Mième' [sic] to report generally on the West Coast of Africa."* Ampthill had omitted to note the significance of the fact that Bismarck had placed Angra Pequena under German protection and thus inaugurated a colonial policy on 24 April 1884, over a month before this despatch was written. It is clear that the British Ambassador failed to realize what was going on. He was ill at this time, in May he had been confined to bed with a feverish attack, and in August he had to request leave of absence for reasons of health. He died on 25 August 1884, before he could get away from Berlin (2). It cannot be doubted that his failing health affected his conduct of business at this critical time. His subordinate at the embassy wrote that "from certain things he said lately I now think he himself felt his useful career was coming to an end,"† and Count Herbert Bismarck wrote to Granville that if Ampthill "had not been ailing and low spirited for some time past he might have kept our relations free from every sort of uneasiness."‡

It is unfortunate for Granville that his two chief sources of information as to Bismarck's intentions, the German embassy in London and the British embassy in Berlin, should have failed him at this point. The preconceived view which he held, that Bismarck was not seriously interested in Angra Pequena, induced him to refrain from action himself, and to give the colonial office its own way entirely. But, no matter how much Ampthill and Münster were to be blamed for not seeing things clearly, or Bismarck for not making things clear to them, it is difficult to excuse Granville for not answering Bismarck's precise questions as to England's title to Angra

* 30 May 1884. Lord Ampthill to Lord Granville. British Blue Book, (C. 4190), No. 58, Enclosure 1.

† 28 August 1884. C. S. Scott to Sanderson. Private. Private Granville MSS, G.D. 29/179.

‡ 30 August 1884. Count Herbert Bismarck to Lord Granville. Private. *Die Grosse Politik,* IV, No. 752.

Pequena, or for allowing the colonial office to interpret these questions as an invitation to annex the territory.

Since it was the colonial office, and not the foreign office, that played the decisive part in the early stages of the negotiations, it is important to follow the activities of this department, and to trace the influences at work upon it. During the last months of 1883 it was principally occupied with the attempt to establish a claim to Angra Pequena. Unfortunately for the British Government, Bismarck had been quite correct in stating, in the note presented by Münster on 31 December 1883, that in papers laid before Parliament it had been made clear that the territory in which Angra Pequena was situated was outside the limits of the Queen's sovereignty. England had not the shadow of a claim to this territory. The evidence was all the other way. In 1867 the British Government had expressly refused to annex the country to the northward of the Cape Colony.* In November 1880 inquiry was made through the German ambassador as to whether England would extend protection to the representatives of the Rhenish Missionary Society in Namaqualand and Hereroland.† Lord Granville consulted the colonial secretary, and replied that the latter was certain the Cape Colony would be ready to protect German subjects so far as was in their power, but that England could not be made responsible for anything that happened outside of British territory, "which includes only Walfisch Bay and a very small region in its vicinity."‡ Again, in instructions to the governor of the Cape Colony in December 1880, which were subsequently published in a British Blue Book, Lord Kimberley, the colonial secretary, had stated: "Her Majesty's Government are of opinion that the Orange River should be maintained as the north-western limit of the Cape Colony, and they will give no countenance

* 23 August 1867. Duke of Buckingham and Chandos to Governor Sir P. E. Wodehouse. British Blue Book, (C. 4265), Appendix I.

† 4 November 1880. Instructions to Count Münster. German White Book, *Angra Pequena*, No. I.

‡ 29 November 1880. Lord Granville to Count Münster. German White Book, *Angra Pequena*, No. II, Enclosure.

to schemes for the extension of British jurisdiction over Great Namaqualand and Damaraland."*

But when, in the autumn of 1883, Bismarck began to question the English rights to Angra Pequena, the colonial office at once reversed its former policy, and made a tremendous effort to build up a claim to that territory. The ministers of the Cape Colony had pointed out, in a minute of 31 October 1883, that as far back as 1796 a Captain Alexander of the *Star* had landed at Angra Pequena and other points along the coast, taking possession of them in the King's name.† Later it was also reported from the Cape that Angra Pequena had been annexed by Captain Forsyth of the *Valorous* in 1866.‡ But both these claims proved to be invalid. Lord Derby had to admit that in "the Letters Patent annexing the various islands to the Cape, no reference is made to the Harbour; and it would appear therefore that Captain Forsyth's act, so far as it related to the Harbour itself, did not receive Her Majesty's confirmation. It might perhaps however, be quoted as a prior claim against that of Mr. Lüderitz, and in any case it would seem scarcely probable that the German Government would wish to insist upon so limited a sovereignty as that over a bay of small extent, the islands in which belong to another Power."§

An appeal was now made to the admiralty for any information they might have as to the proceedings of Her Majesty's ships at Angra Pequena.|| The answer was, however, disappointing. A ship had called at Angra Pequena in 1851, but had not taken possession. Another ship took possession of Ichabo Island off the coast in 1861, but did not even call at Angra Pequena. The *Valorous* had indeed annexed several

* 30 December 1880. Lord Kimberley to Governor Sir H. Robinson. British Blue Book, (C. 2754), presented January 1881.

† 31 October 1883. Minute. Ministers to Administrator. British Blue Book, (C. 4190), No. 31, Enclosure 2.

‡ 13 November 1883. Officer administering the government to Lord Derby. *Ibid.*, No. 33.

§ 12 December 1883. Colonial office to foreign office. F.O. 64/1101.

|| 12 December 1883. Colonial office to admirality. British Blue Book, (C. 4190), No. 34.

other islands off the coast in 1866, but it had not been reported that Captain Forsyth had made any annexations on the mainland.* The colonial office wrote back to ask if the admiralty had any record of the visit of the *Star* to Angra Pequena in 1796.† In reply, the admiralty sent the report which was made of this visit at the time.‡ Captain Alexander had touched at Angra Pequena, and had taken possession in the name of the British Crown. But, according to Derby's later statement in the House of Lords, "as that transaction took place 90 years ago, and was not followed by any notification to Foreign Powers, the question might fairly be raised how far a nominal claim of that kind would be held to be valid now."§

There was a good deal behind this sudden burst of activity on the part of the colonial office. Lord Derby was highly susceptible to pressure, especially from the colonies, and the Cape Colony was developing an increasing interest in Angra Pequena and the German activities there. As early as 17 September 1883, there was sent to the colonial office in London an extract from a report on the proceedings of German traders at Angra Pequena, and on an interview with Lüderitz, who had expressed his anxiety to respect all preëxisting rights.|| This was supplemented by a long minute dated 31 October 1883, which reached London on 28 November. It discussed in detail "the complications which may arise from the creation of a rival interest in a country which has hitherto been considered as a kind of commercial dependency of this Colony." The Colony laid great stress on the control of the arms traffic, and considered "that the establishment of a trading station of this kind, must put an end to all hopes of any control over the import of arms and ammunition to South-

* 27 December 1883. Admiralty to colonial office. British Blue Book, (C. 4190), No. 36, Enclosure.

† 5 January 1884. Colonial office to admiralty. *Ibid.*, No. 37.

‡ 23 January 1884. Admiralty to colonial office. F.O. 64/1102. The enclosed report is in British Blue Book, (C. 4190), footnote on p. 28.

§ 19 May 1884. *Hansard Parliamentary Debates,* 3rd Series, CCLXXXVIII, 646.

|| 17 September 1883. Officer administering the government to Lord Derby. British Blue Book, (C. 4190), No. 17.

western Africa, while, in other respects, the establishment of what is practically a free port will lead to a very great disturbance of the ordinary trade which has hitherto existed with the Colony. At the same time, the creation of separate proprietary rights may very possibly tend to complications and disputes, of an extremely inconvenient kind, among the different European interests on the coast." All these considerations induced the ministers of the Cape Colony to make a broad hint in the direction of annexation. "They would venture to express their opinion that the present would be a suitable occasion to define more accurately than hitherto the position of this coast with regard to the exercise of sovereign rights."*

With this minute was sent a communication from the British trader, Captain J. Spence, who feared that losses to his firm might occur if the Germans were allowed to take possession of Angra Pequena without some protection to existing British interests being guaranteed. He did not ask for British protection, but, on the contrary, begged for a recommendation to the German Government.† Captain Spence was a member of the firm of De Pass, Spence, and Co., whose representative in London, Daniel De Pass, addressed to the colonial office all through the negotiations a steady stream of protests against the German activities. There does not appear to have been entire accord between the two members of the firm, because Spence never asked for British protection, nor did he object to German annexation, but only to the private act of Lüderitz of erecting buildings on a grant of land belonging to his firm. He wrote to the German consul in Cape Town: "I have no objection whatever to the German Government annexing this territory and I am quite certain if they do my rights will be fully acknowledged as established as herein stated."‡

* 31 October 1883. Minute. Ministers to Administrator. British Blue Book, (C. 4190), No. 31, Enclosure 2.

† 29 October 1883. Captain J. Spence to J. X. Merriman. British Blue Book, (C. 4190), No. 31, Enclosure 1.

‡ 25 September 1883. Captain J. Spence to German consul in Cape Town. Copy. Reichsarchiv, Vermischtes Südwestafrika I.

In a further minute, of 30 January 1884, the ministers of the Cape Colony desired "to put on record their opinion that, in the present circumstances of South Africa, the interests of order and civilization would be best served by the annexation to the Empire of the remainder of the coast from the Portuguese possessions to the Orange River, and by the issue of a commission to the Officer who may be charged with the administration of the Government of the Cape of Good Hope as Governor of the territory in a manner similar to that which was followed in the case of the territories of Tembuland and St. John's River, leaving the question of the settlement of the amount of effective control and the provision to be made in that behalf to be arranged between Her Majesty's Government and the Government of the Colony."*

The representations of the Cape Colony were vigorously seconded by Mr. Scanlen in London, who spared no effort to impress the colonial point of view upon Lord Derby. He wrote home that he had "called attention to matters on the West Coast. Lord Derby thinks that the German Government has no intention of establishing a Colony in any part of South Africa, and admitted that it would not be advisable for Great Britain to allow any European power to get a footing anywhere there as on the East Coast."† Sir Hercules Robinson, the governor of the Cape Colony, was also in London in the last months of 1883, and remained there until March 1884.‡ He too, played a part in the negotiations.

The result of the inquiry into the title of England to Angra Pequena had been disappointing, and Lord Derby now took advantage of Robinson's presence in London to ask his advice. He sent him the communications that had come from the admiralty, showing the weakness of England's claim, and sent him also a translation of Münster's note of 31 December 1883. Derby wished to be informed whether, in the opinion

* 30 January 1884. Minute. Ministers to Administrator. British Blue Book, (C. 4190), No. 42, Enclosure.

† T. Scanlen to J. X. Merriman. Sir Perceval Laurence: *Life of John Xavier Merriman*, p. 85.

‡ *The Times:* 11 February 1884, p. 8, col. 1; 7 March 1884, p. 8, col. 6.

of Sir Hercules Robinson, he was "right in concluding that there is no prospect of the Cape Government offering to undertake the control of Angra Pequena; as in such case it would appear difficult to resist the representation of the German Government that, failing other protection for German subjects at that place, they must assume jurisdiction over it."* On 1 February 1884, Sir Hercules Robinson replied, intimating that he could not give an answer himself, but recommending that the Cape Government should be consulted, as Mr. Scanlen had by this time returned to Cape Town (3). Accordingly, on 3 February, Derby addressed a telegraphic inquiry to the officer administering the government of the Cape Colony, in almost the same words that had been used in the letter to Robinson.† The reply from the Cape was: "Ministers ask matter be kept open, pending Cabinet meeting here. Premier away."‡ No further reply was sent until the following May, when Lord Derby brought the matter up again. The position of the ministers of the Cape Colony was a delicate one. They had presented a minute on 30 January 1884, recommending in very definite terms the annexation of the coastline of South West Africa, and suggesting that the questions of the amount of effective control and the provision to be made for it be left open. This minute had been sent to London by mail, was on its way there when Derby telegraphed, and arrived on 23 February. The ministers knew that a full statement of their views on the desirability of annexing Angra Pequena would soon reach London. Meanwhile they were extremely reluctant to assume the responsibility for the control of this territory because of the financial burden which would go with it, and it was not improbably for this reason that they hesitated to reply to the direct invitation Derby had given them to undertake the

* 29 January 1884. Colonial office to Sir Hercules Robinson. Copy. F.O. 64/1102.

† 5 February 1884. Lord Derby to officer administering the government at Cape Town, reporting his telegram of 3 February. British Blue Book, (C. 4190), No. 39.

‡ 6 February 1884. Telegram. Officer administering the government at Cape Town to Lord Derby. *Ibid.*, No. 40.

control. Merriman wrote to the Cape agent in London: "We have asked Lord Derby by minute to formally annex the coast leaving the question of the payment for the form of Govt. open. He now naturally declines unless we promise to actually annex the coast which, in the present state of our Colonial affairs, we are in no position to give a pledge about. . . ."* The result was that the Cape allowed the matter to drift, and Bismarck received no answer to the questions he had put to the British Government.

Lord Derby's policy requires some explanation. When Münster's note of 31 December 1883 was sent to him, on 19 January 1884, he was already in a position to answer the inquiries contained therein as to England's claim to Angra Pequena, for by this time England's claims to Angra Pequena had all been investigated, and found to be invalid. But, instead of returning a direct answer to Germany, Derby asked the Cape Colony if it would assume control over the place, as it might "be difficult otherwise to resist the representation made by the German Government" that they would have to assume jurisdiction themselves. Derby, like Granville, was acting upon a preconceived opinion as to Germany's intentions, and his opinion was probably based on the same grounds, the German communication of February 1883, and the language held by Ampthill and Münster. And, since he was already convinced that Bismarck was by inclination strongly opposed to colonies, he might easily have been misled by the words in Münster's note in which it was asked what institutions England possessed at Angra Pequena "which would secure such legal protection for German subjects in their commercial enterprises and justly won acquisitions, as would relieve the Empire from the duty of providing itself directly for its subjects in that territory the protection of which they may stand in need."† No doubt Derby was quite sincere when he wrote later to Sir Hercules Robinson: "But

* 6 February 1884. J. X. Merriman to Captain Mills, the Cape agent in London. Sir Perceval Laurence: *Life of John Xavier Merriman,* p. 89.

† 31 December 1883. Count Münster to Lord Granville. Translation. British Blue Book, (C. 4190), No. 38, Enclosure.

it appeared to us from the language used in the Ambassador's note of December 1883, that such a proceeding [i.e., independent action on the part of the German Government] would only be resorted to as an alternative, from which Germany would willingly be relieved by action on the part of the British Government. I fully understood that the choice was before us of annexing the country or acquiescing in a German annexation."* There is not sufficient evidence for believing that the colonial office was trying to steal a march on Germany, and to present a *fait accompli* while the negotiations were still going on. But Derby had ample evidence that the Cape Colony was much interested in the territory in question, and for this reason he very much preferred that England should take charge of the place, if that could possibly be managed. He was not a clear thinker, and though he vaguely realized the German Government had some desire to annex Angra Pequena, he apparently believed that they did not care much about it, and could be persuaded to accept either solution. However, even if Bismarck's ultimate intentions had not been made manifest, the German inquiries as to England's title were extremely precise, and could not be answered simply by a British annexation. Derby failed to appreciate the situation and probably never dreamed he was provoking a quarrel with Germany. He was, in fact, strongly opposed to intervention in European affairs. It was his opinion that "the less we are mixed up in the sanguinary muddle of Continental diplomacy the better for England," and he regretted that England was not "in the happy position of the United States, who can afford to have no foreign policy."† By his naïve and injudicious handling of the German colonial affair Derby brought upon England the very calamity that he would naturally have been most anxious to avoid.

Meanwhile things were developing in Germany. In Janu-

* 4 December 1884. Lord Derby to Sir Hercules Robinson. British Blue Book, (C. 4265).

† 10 October 1885. Speech by Lord Derby at Blackburn. *Speeches of Lord Derby*, II, 136.

ary the German gunboat *Nautilus* was ordered to Angra Pequena to report, and its arrival at Cape Town caused a flurry among the colonial ministers, who begged that word be telegraphed to London that the *Nautilus* was going to Angra Pequena to raise the German flag. The officer administering the government consulted Lippert, the German consul, and received from him an assurance that the commander of the *Nautilus* had no intention of raising the German flag and that this event would not take place. To the prime minister of the Cape Colony Lippert gave the additional explanation that the *Nautilus* was instructed only to make a report (4). His statements seem to have relieved the Cape authorities, and probably contributed to their reluctance to take action during the following months.

Lippert's report on these events reached Berlin in February, and was sent on to Münster with instructions to take no new step for the present, as the report of the *Nautilus* was still being awaited. But it was stated that if, besides handing in the note of 31 December 1883, Münster had discussed the matter verbally in London, the German Government would like him to report on it (5).

Bismarck now permitted the subject of Angra Pequena to lapse for a while, and turned his attention to another matter. It has been related how he took up the land claims of evicted German subjects in the Fiji Islands, and pressed the British Government for a reconsideration of them by a mixed commission. On 9 January 1884, in reply to a new request from the German Government, the British Government submitted a lengthy memorandum, explaining in detail why it could not comply with Bismarck's wishes.* On 4 April 1884 instructions were sent to Count Münster to present certain complaints on the bad treatment of German subjects in the Fiji Islands. This Fiji question was used to open a much larger one, which may be considered as a suggestion for a general understanding between England and Germany in the future.

* 9 January 1884. Lord Granville to Count Münster. German White Book, *Deutsche Land-Reklamationen auf Fidji,* No. 24, Enclosures 1 and 2.

In the instructions to Münster the possibility was put forward of a change in German policy if England did not prove herself to be more accommodating. It was argued that Germany had been very obliging to England in all great political questions, and had avoided everything that could cause her embarrassment. But if now, in a case where the right was unquestionably on her side, Germany could not even obtain a just examination of her demands, England might have cause to ask herself whether she could count on Germany's continued support. Germany's attitude to England had been friendly because she had not needed English support in matters of like importance, but the conclusion was not to be drawn that Germany would neglect the justified claims of her subjects merely out of good will towards England; on the contrary, an unfriendly and unfair treatment of German nationals must necessarily affect Germany's political relations with England.* The enclosed note, dealing with Fiji, was handed in on 8 April by Count Münster.† Granville replied, promising that the matter should receive his "immediate and attentive consideration."‡

The report of the *Nautilus* reached the German foreign office in March 1884.§ The commander had visited Angra Pequena, had seen the harbor, had talked to Lüderitz and inspected his two deeds of purchase, and reported very favorably on the soundness of his title and the possibilities of his enterprise.||

On 8 April 1884 Herr von Kusserow of the German foreign office submitted for Bismarck's consideration a lengthy *Promemoria* on Angra Pequena. Kusserow pointed out that no report had been received from Münster as to the execu-

* 4 April 1884. Count Hatzfeldt to Count Münster. *Die Grosse Politik,* IV, No. 736.

† 8 April 1884. Count Münster to Lord Granville. German White Book, *Deutsche Land-Reklamationen auf Fidji,* No. 25.

‡ 10 April 1884. Lord Granville to Count Münster. Draft. F.O. 64/1108.

§ 7 March 1884. German admiralty to German foreign office. Reichsarchiv, Vermischtes Südwestafrika II.

|| 27 January 1884. Aschenborn, commander of the *Nautilus,* to German admiralty. German White Book, *Angra Pequena,* No. 11.

tion of his instructions of 27 December 1883, but on the other hand a favorable report had come in from the commander of the *Nautilus,* and Lüderitz, recently returned from Angra Pequena, had asked again for German protection. Lüderitz hoped that the German Government, even if it would not undertake a protectorate, would find some way to prevent the annexation of his territory by another power. Von Kusserow thought this object might be achieved by means of a treaty with the native chieftain, in which Germany should make it clear to the natives as well as to other powers that she looked upon that territory as independent. This was a very moderate proposal for Kusserow to make, for he was an ardent colonial enthusiast. His moderation suggests how little Bismarck's subordinates were in touch with what was going on in the chancellor's mind at the moment. Kusserow even thought it necessary to add that the treaty with the native chieftain must express the fact that the territory remained under this chieftain's sovereignty. Bismarck, however, questioned this procedure. "Under German protection?" he wrote in the margin, and opposite the passage where Lüderitz asked the German Government to prevent annexation by other powers, Bismarck wrote: "for that we must either take possession, or recognise Lüderitz as sovereign." He agreed to von Kusserow's suggestion that the Reichsjustizamt be consulted in regard to granting a "royal charter" on the English model (6). In other words, Bismarck had come to the conclusion that Lüderitz should receive something more than mere consular protection; he now appears to have considered placing Angra Pequena under German protection, and giving it a "royal charter," and he even mentioned the possibility of annexation.

Bismarck's next step was taken on 24 April 1884. According to information received from Herr Lüderitz, the authorities in Cape Town doubted whether his acquisitions north of the Orange River, i.e., at Angra Pequena, had claim to German protection. Although Münster's note of 31 December 1883 was still unanswered, Bismarck took the initiative at this point, and telegraphed to the German consul in Cape Town on 24 April, instructing him to declare officially that Lüderitz and his establishments were under the protection of the German Empire.* On the same day, Bismarck telegraphed to the German ambassador in London, asking him to inform Lord Granville of the instructions which had been sent to Cape Town.† This communication was made to Granville by the German chargé d'affaires, Count Vitzthum, since the ambassador, Münster, was away in Germany on leave. In reply Granville stated that he would place himself in communication with the colonial office.‡ He does not appear to have realized the significance of Bismarck's act, and it was not until some time later that he was made to see that the possibility of a British annexation of Angra Pequena had now been excluded.

* 24 April 1884. Bismarck to Consul Lippert. Telegram. German White Book, *Angra Pequena,* No. 12.

† 24 April 1884. Bismarck to German ambassador in London. Telegram. German White Book, *Angra Pequena,* No. 13.

‡ 25 April 1884. Lord Granville to Lord Ampthill. British Blue Book, (C. 4190), No. 43, Enclosure.

NOTES

1. The four following passages further illustrate the type of report that Ampthill was continually sending home:

18 September 1880. Lord Odo Russell to Lord Granville. British Blue Book, (C. 4190), No. 3, Enclosure.

"Herr von Weber's plan will not meet with any support either at the hands of the German Government or on the part of the German parliament, while German emigrants feel more attracted by a republican form of Government than by that of a Crown Colony.

"The German Government feel more the want of soldiers than of colonies, and consequently discourage emigration.

"The German parliament has marked its disinclination to acquire distant dependencies however advantageous to German enterprise, by the rejection of the Samoa Bill.

"Under present circumstances therefore the plan for a German Colony in South Africa has no prospect of success."

14 February 1883. Lord Ampthill to Lord Granville. No. 59. F.O. 64/1101.

This despatch describes a meeting of the German Colonization Society in the Reichstag Buildings on 10 February 1883. The despatch ends: "I should add that the meeting was not attended by any Member of the Government."

31 August 1883. Sir John Walsham (the British chargé d'affaires in Berlin) to Lord Granville. British Blue Book, (C. 4190), No. 12, Enclosure.

"In alluding to this purchase, [i.e., Lüderitz's purchase of Angra Pequena] the Press expresses its satisfaction at learning that the German Government have accorded protection to Mr. Lüderitz's undertaking, but it is also clear that the amount of protection to be afforded is precisely what would be granted to any other subject of the Empire who had settled abroad and acquired property. It would be a mistake to suppose that the Imperial Government have any present intention of establishing Crown colonies, or of imitating, as the Press adds, the practice adopted by France of assuming a protectorate over any territory acquired by a French traveller or explorer.

"The German Government are opposed to any plan which might hamper their foreign relations, and I believe that what Lord Ampthill stated in his despatch, to which I have referred [the despatch of 18 September 1880], is as true to-day as it was in 1880."

8 April 1884. Lord Ampthill to Lord Granville. No. 92. F.O. 64/1102.

"With reference to my despatch No. 59 of February 14th, 1883, and to Sir John Walsham's No. 254 of August 31, 1883, I have the honour to report to your Lordship that a new colonization Society has just been started at Berlin with the avowed object of founding German Agricultural and Trading Colonies.

". . . There is no reason to suppose that the German Government will be more disposed to lend its countenance to the efforts of this Society than it has been in the case of similar movements in the past."

2. The following quotations will indicate the stages of Ampthill's decline in health which are mentioned in the text:

5 May 1884. Lord Ampthill to Lord Granville. No. 114. F.O. 64/1050.

"I have the honour to report that I have returned to Berlin from Darmstadt, but being unfortunately confined to bed in consequence of a chill and feverish attack, I have requested Mr. Scott to continue for the present to attend to the current business of the Embassy."

Lord Ampthill's illness is also reported in *The Times,* 7 May 1884, p. 7, col. 2.

The Times, 10 May 1884, p. 7, col. 3.

"Lord Ampthill himself is still confined to his room, and is quite unable to receive visitors."

16 August 1884. Lord Ampthill to Lord Granville. No. 222. F.O. 64/1051.

"If not inconvenient, I should be much obliged to your Lordship for leave to absent myself from my post during the recess, partly for health and partly for private affairs in England."

16 August 1884. Lord Ampthill to Lord Granville. Private. Private Granville MSS, G.D. 29/178.

"My Doctor will not let me off Carlsbad this year, so I am going to ask you to let me go to Bohemia first and Bedfordshire afterwards during the recess."

Lord Granville acceded to the request for leave of absence in a despatch of 21 August 1884, No. 240. Draft is in F.O. 64/1048.

Lord Ampthill's death, on 25 August 1884, was reported in a despatch of the same date from Mr. C. S. Scott of the British embassy in Berlin to Lord Granville, No. 231. F.O. 64/1051.

3. 1 February 1884. Sir Hercules Robinson in London to colonial office. Copy. F.O. 64/1102.

"In reply to your letter of the 29th January, enclosing documents with reference to the rights of sovereignty over the Bay of Angra Pequena and adjacent territory, I would suggest that, as Mr. Scanlen has by this time returned to Cape Town, a cable message should be sent to the Officer Administering the Government as follows:—'Is there any prospect of the Cape

Government undertaking the control of Angra Pequena, as, if not, it would be difficult to resist the representation of the German Government that, failing other protection for German subjects at that place, they must assume jurisdiction over it?'

"The papers which accompanied your letter are herewith returned."

4. 22 January 1884. Lippert, the German consul in Cape Town, to the German foreign office. German White Book, *Angra Pequena,* No. 10. Several paragraphs are omitted from the White Book, of which the two following are referred to in the text. They are quoted from the original in the Reichsarchiv, Vermischtes Südwestafrika II.

"Das Ministerium habe ihn [the officer administering the government] ersucht, der englischen Regierung zu telegraphiren, dass S.M.S. "Nautilus" nach Angra Pequena ginge, um wie er voraussetze, die deutsche Flagge dorten aufzuziehen.

"Da ich mit dem Commandanten des genannten Schiffes auch hierüber Rücksprache genommen hatte, so konnte ich Seine Excellenz versichern, dass dies durchaus nicht beabsichtigt sei und auch nicht stattfinden werde, und schien diese Mittheilung sowohl ihn als auch bei einer späteren Unterredung die ich in Abwesenheit des Colonial-Secretary's mit dem vorsitzenden Minister hatte, den letzteren sehr zu befriedigen.—Ich gab an dass S. M. Schiff nur beauftragt sei, über die Verhältnisse von Angra Pequena Bericht zu erstatten."

5. 22 February 1884. Instructions to Count Münster. Draft. Reichsarchiv, Vermischtes Südwestafrika II.

". . . Zweck dieses Erlasses ist nicht, Ew. pp. in diesem Augenblick zu einer erneuten Anregung der Sache bei der grossbritannischen Regierung zu veranlassen, da wir hinzu eventuell den noch ausstehenden Bericht des Kommandanten S. M. Kanonenboot "Nautilus" zu verwerthen uns vorbehalten.

"Falls jedoch Ew. pp. s. Zt. ausser der Uebermittelung der Note an Lord Granville in Gemässheit des Erlasses vom 27. Dezember v. Js. die Angelegenheit dort mündlich erörtert haben sollten, würde mir von Interesse sein, Ew. pp. gefällige Mittheilungen hierüber zu erhalten."

6. 8 April 1884. *Promemoria betreffend Angra Pequena,* by Herr von Kusserow, with marginal comments by Prince Bismarck. Reichsarchiv, Vermischtes Südwestafrika II.

The *Promemoria* begins by discussing the instructions to Count Münster of 31 December 1883.

"Eine Antwort hierauf haben wir bis heute nicht erhalten; auch fehlt noch ein Bericht des Kaiserlichen Botschafters über mündliche Verwerthung der Fidji-Angelegenheit im Sinne des Erlasses vom 27. Dezember.

"Dagegen liegen vor: 1. ein durch Karten illustrirter Bericht des Commandanten S. M. Kbt. 'Nautilus' vom 27. Januar d.J. in welchem sich derselbe über die Rechtstitel des Herrn Lüderitz und die Bedeutung seines Unternehmens sehr günstig ausspricht, und 2. eine Eingabe des kürzlich von Angra Pequena zurückgekehrten Herrn Lüderitz vom 21. v. Mts., in welcher er, unter Einreichung beweiskräftiger Urkunden für sein Recht auf das volle Eigenthum an einem 900 Quadratmeilen betragenden . . . Gebiete, um den Schutz des Reichs für sein Unternehmen bittet.

". . . Eines schriftlichen Antrages über die *Form* des zu gewährenden Schutzes hat er [i.e. Lüderitz] sich enthalten zu sollen geglaubt, weil er nach den ihm gemachten Andeutungen besorgt, dass sein Wunsch wegen Inbesitznahme seines Gebietes oder Uebernahme eines Protektorats über dasselbe durch das Reich sich nicht erfüllen werde. Er hofft aber, dass die Kaiserl.

Regierung irgend eine Form finden werde, um die Annexion des fraglichen Gebietes durch eine andere Macht zu verhüten. (Bismarck: dazu mussten wir entweder Besitz ergreifen, oder Lüderitz als Souverain anerkennen.)

". . . Zugleich mit Verleihung einer solchen Konzession an Herrn Lüderitz, sowie auch in dem Falle, dass hiervon abgesehn werden sollte, würde durch den Abschluss eines Vertrages zwischen dem Reich und dem Häuptling von Bethanien, womit wohl Generalkonsul Dr. Nachtigal betraut werden könnte, sowohl den Eingeborenen wie dritten Nationen gegenüber zu bekunden sein, dass wir jenes Gebiet als ein unabhängiges ansehen. (Bismarck: als deutsches Schutzland?)

". . . Der Vertrag müsste aussprechen, das auch für das an Lüderitz verkaufte Gebiet die Landeshoheit bei dem Häuptlinge von Bethanien verbleibt, (Bismarck: unter deutschem Schutz?) und dieser müsste die Ausübung der Zollhoheit dort selbst übernehmen, oder Herrn Lüderitz hierzu ermächtigen; das Nähere würde gleichfalls im Vertrage festzusetzen sein.

". . . 2. Sollten Ew. Durchlaucht geneigt sein, dem Gedanken, wegen Verleihung einer der Form der Englischen 'Royal Charter' nachzubildenden Konzession näher zu treten, so könnte hierüber vielleicht zunächst vertraulich mit dem Reichsjustizamt konferirt werden? (Bismarck: ja. besser vielleicht noch Vertrag mit dem Häuptling.)"

The last three paragraphs, of those quoted above, have been published in Dr. Alfred Zimmerman's *Geschichte der Deutschen Kolonialpolitik,* pp. 66-8.

IV

MÜNSTER'S MISSION

BY 27 April 1884, Count Münster had returned from his fortnight's visit to Germany and resumed control of the embassy in London.* In the month that followed he developed, by order of his government, overtures to England which represented a new departure on the side of Germany. Apparently Bismarck considered that, by his declaration of 24 April that Angra Pequena stood under German protection, he had settled that question, at least for the time being, and was free to take up a new subject. He appears to have believed that, by this declaration, he had excluded the possibility of the annexation of Angra Pequena to the British Empire.

But whether or not Bismarck realized that his statement was open to misconstruction, there is no doubt that it was, for the term "protection" was an extremely vague one, and Bismarck himself appears to have attached different meanings to it at different times. At the beginning of 1883 he used the term, in connection with the undertaking of Herr Lüderitz, to denote the assistance of the nearest German consul and the occasional visit of a German warship. But in April 1884 he had it in mind to grant the settlement at Angra Pequena a "royal charter" on the English model, a step which was so far-reaching as to render impossible the exercise of sovereignty at that place by any other power. But he had not yet decided to take the further step of founding a colony, and when Lüderitz offered to appoint and maintain the necessary officials himself, Bismarck assented (1).

The significance which Bismarck attached to his declara-

* 27 April 1884. Count Münster to Lord Granville, announcing his return to London. F.O. 64/1069.

tion was not, however, wholly clear to the English authorities. It does not seem to have occurred to any of them that Bismarck intended to claim exclusive control over the coast of South West Africa, and to exclude other powers from it. Mr. Scanlen, the Cape premier, received the message of the German consul on 24 April "with some astonishment as to what could have impelled the Imperial Government to this communication."* When the governor, Sir Hercules Robinson, forwarded the German consul's letter to London, the only comment he made was that he had not yet heard from the ministers of the Cape Colony whether they would accept Derby's invitation of 3 February 1884 to take control of Angra Pequena.† Similarly, when the German chargé d'affaires informed Lord Granville of the instructions that had been sent to the German consul in Cape Town, Lord Granville replied only that he would communicate with the colonial office."‡ In making this communication, the foreign office begged that Lord Derby might be moved "to take, without delay, such steps as will enable Lord Granville to explain the circumstances to the German Government."§ On 2 May Sir George Dallas, of the foreign office, took the further step of making private inquiries at the colonial office. He discovered that "the question has been hung up in consequence of a telegram from the Cape requesting that action might be suspended, but that the question will now be again taken into consideration."‖ The telegram referred to must be the one of 6 February 1884, described in the preceding chapter. Apparently the colonial office had, since then, allowed the matter to drift. As a result of the renewed request from the foreign office a further telegram was, on 7 May, addressed to the Cape, saying that it was "necessary to tell German Minister what is intended by Her Majesty's Government respecting Angra Pe-

* 28 April 1884. Lippert, the German consul in Cape Town, to Prince Bismarck. German White Book, *Angra Pequena,* No. 18.

† 29 April 1884. Sir Hercules Robinson to Lord Derby. British Blue Book, (C. 4190), No. 50.

‡ 25 April 1884. Lord Granville to Lord Ampthill. *Ibid.,* No. 43, Enclosure.

§ 25 April 1884. Foreign office to colonial office. *Ibid.,* No. 43.

‖ 2 May 1884. Memorandum by Sir George Dallas. F.O. 64/1102.

quena, and if Colonial Government desires that it should be under British jurisdiction they should immediately express readiness accept responsibility and cost."* But on that very day the government of the Cape Colony resigned in consequence of a defeat in the House of Assembly,† and it was not until 12 May that the formation of a new government was announced.‡ The result was a further delay in answering the inquiries of the colonial office. On 15 May the governor telegraphed that the new cabinet was "making inquiries *re* Angra Pequena, and hope to send definite reply within ten days."§ By the time the promised reply reached England, two weeks later, there had been many new developments, and the situation was completely altered.

But Bismarck, of course, did not know that all this was going on, and apparently it did not even occur to him that his declaration of 24 April had not been explicit. Although no reply had as yet been vouchsafed to Münster's note of 31 December 1883, Bismarck appears to have thought that by now he had brought the Angra Pequena question up to a point where it was possible to open a new and more general line of policy.

This new development had been foreshadowed in the instructions to Münster of 4 April 1884, where a hint had been given that if England did not prove more accommodating in regard to Fiji, she might not be able to reckon in the future upon Germany's support for her policy in Egypt. Münster reverted to this subject when he called on Granville shortly after his return to London at the end of April. When Granville then expressed his appreciation of Germany's friendly policy in regard to Egypt, the German ambassador took advantage of this opportunity to remark that Bismarck thought he had not found in all questions the same obligingness on the English side. Lord Granville regretted this, and said that

* 7 May 1884. Lord Derby to Sir Hercules Robinson. Telegram. British Blue Book, (C. 4190), No. 45.

† *The Times.* 8 May 1884, p. 5, col. 4.

‡ *The Times.* 13 May 1884, p. 5, col. 4.

§ 15 May 1884. Sir Hercules Robinson to Lord Derby. Telegram. British Blue Book, (C. 4190), No. 48.

it was his most sincere wish to achieve the best possible understanding between the two countries.*

In a despatch of 5 May 1884, Bismarck expressed his pleasure that Granville appreciated the friendly policy of Germany, and declared that he was ready to continue this policy provided that a similar cordiality manifested itself on the English side. "An early opportunity for the latter," he wrote, "might be afforded by giving attention to our grievances regarding the treatment of German nationals in the South Seas and by showing greater consideration for our trade interests in Africa." The question of Angra Pequena was, for the moment, entirely dropped, except for this brief reference to Africa, and Bismarck confined himself to the demand for fair treatment for Germans trading overseas and freedom for German commerce. He protested against the recent Anglo-Portuguese treaty in regard to the Congo, on the ground that it was injurious to German trade, and he also mentioned Fiji again, as well as Little Popo, where Germany had trading interests. Bismarck's object appears to have been to achieve a sort of general understanding by which, in return for supporting England in Egypt, he would receive, not assistance in furthering his colonial projects, but equitable treatment by England of German trading interests and German citizens overseas.

In the same despatch. Bismarck brought up another suggestion, which was that, in order to strengthen the good relations between the two countries, England should cede to Germany the island of Heligoland. In British possession, he argued, this island was of little value. But Germany, if she owned it, would not object to the expense of providing it with a harbor of safety, which would be a great convenience to England as well as to other nations. An agreement by treaty through which the island was ceded to Germany, perhaps with the condition of building a harbor of safety there, would make a very desirable impression upon German public opin-

* 29 April 1884. Count Münster to Prince Bismarck. *Die Grosse Politik,* IV, No. 737.

ion. Bismarck then plunged into a discussion of the value which German friendship could have for England. He pointed out that Germany's bearing towards England's rivals was of greater importance to England than Heligoland and all trade rivalries in distant seas put together. Thus the considerations brought forward in this despatch amounted to an offer, rather than a request. He asked Münster for his opinion as to whether the present time was a favorable one for discussing these matters with Lord Granville.*

Münster replied to the despatch of 5 May with enthusiasm. He wrote that he thought the acquisition of Heligoland would be most advantageous, and very popular in Germany, that there was some hope of the British Government's agreeing to it, and that the moment was favorable for opening the discussion. To the other points of Bismarck's despatch Münster paid little attention. He mentioned the protection that Bismarck wished to give to German traders, only to say that this, coupled with the acquisition of Heligoland, would make it easier to bring public opinion to a more correct view of oversea affairs than existed in Germany at present. Münster explained that he was referring to the well-meant but "unpractical and immature" colonial attempts which had led to the foundation of societies. His criticism indicates that he, as well as the British Government, had failed to realize the significance of Bismarck's action on 24 April 1884. Besides dismissing Bismarck's wish to afford protection to German trade so briefly, Münster did not even mention England's policy in Egypt, or the possibility of a reversal of German policy in regard to it.†

These two omissions were corrected by Bismarck in his reply on 11 May. He explained that the offer to England should consist in German support in England's political affairs, as well as in the advantages accruing to England from a

* 5 May 1884. Prince Bismarck to Count Münster. *Die Grosse Politik*, IV, No. 738. The passage quoted is taken from the translation of E. T. S. Dugdale: *German Diplomatic Documents, 1871-1914*, I, 170.

† 8 May 1884. Count Münster to Prince Bismarck. *Die Grosse Politik*, IV, No. 739.

harbor in Heligoland. The conditions under which Germany would give this support were that her claims should be satisfied in the South Seas and in Africa, inclusive of the Anglo-Portuguese treaty, and that Heligoland should be ceded. This offer was so much the higher because it involved substantial disadvantages for Germany in her relations with France. He requested Münster to go ahead with the matter as soon as possible.*

Bismarck's corrections seem to have had little effect. On 17 May 1884, Münster broached the subject of Heligoland with Lord Granville in a confidential manner. But while he put forward most of the arguments suggested by Bismarck and dwelt upon the advantage that a harbor of safety there would have for England, he apparently said nothing about Bismarck's desire for the satisfaction of Germany's oversea claims, nor did he mention the possibility of a reversal of German policy, if Bismarck were not satisfied on this score."† There is no evidence that Münster brought forward either of these considerations during May, and Bismarck, writing on 1 June, declared that he had as yet received no report as to whether Münster had placed before Lord Granville the alternatives of treating Germany's oversea claims with justice, or of losing Germany's support in political questions which were of major importance to England.‡

But before these negotiations could be carried any further, certain events in England brought Bismarck's attention back to Angra Pequena. The German activities in Africa had been reported from time to time in the English papers, and on 12 May 1884 the matter was brought up in a question in the House of Lords. Viscount Sidmouth asked whether any correspondence on the subject had taken place with the German Government, and whether any previous rights or claims of

* 11 May 1884. Prince Bismarck to Count Münster. *Die Grosse Politik,* IV, No. 740.

† 17 May 1884. Memorandum by Lord Granville. Lord Edmond Fitzmaurice: *Life of Lord Granville,* II, 351.

‡ 1 June 1884. Prince Bismarck to Count Münster. *Die Grosse Politik,* IV, No. 743.

the British Government had been abandoned. Lord Granville replied that the correspondence was going on at the moment, and therefore could not be produced, but he did go so far as to say: "The German Government has never assumed any sovereignty over any portion of these territories that I am aware of."* An account of this interpellation was sent home by Münster on the following day.†

An even more striking statement from another responsible British minister followed. On 16 May, Lord Derby received at the colonial office a deputation of South African merchants, who urged that the government should not give up Angra Pequena to Germany, and that a larger measure of authority should be established over that territory. Lord Derby replied that the government "had not claimed the place itself as British territory; but we had claimed a sort of general right to exclude foreign Powers from that coast up to the Portuguese territory. The German Government had made various inquiries into the nature of our claims, but so far as the correspondence had yet gone he did not understand that Germany had actually disputed those claims. He apprehended that the question was not really so much one of any intention on the part of the German Government to set up a colony there as an inquiry upon their part whether we claim the possession of the coast, and in that case whether we will give security to the Germans trading or settling there, and if we are either unable or unwilling to give them security whether we shall object to the German Government doing it themselves." The British Government had twice asked the Cape Colony whether they would take over Angra Pequena and the responsibility for the maintenance of order there. The Cape Colony had at first declined because of the expense, and an answer to the second offer had not yet come because of the recent ministerial crisis in the colony.‡ This incident was

* 12 May 1884. *Hansard Parliamentary Debates,* 3rd Series, CCLXXXVIII, pp. 3-5.

† 13 May 1884. Count Münster to Prince Bismarck. Reichsarchiv, Vermischtes Südwestafrika II.

‡ *The Times.* 17 May 1884, p. 9, col. 5.

also fully described by Münster, in a long despatch written on the following day.*

On 19 May 1884, Lord Derby made a similar statement in the House of Lords, in reply to another question from Viscount Sidmouth. He declared that, "although we have not formally claimed the Bay, we have claimed the right to exclude Foreign Powers on the general ground of its nearness to our Settlements, and the absence of any other claims. . . ." The Cape Colony had been invited to take possession of the place, he continued, an answer from them was expected in about ten days, and Her Majesty's Government were waiting for this to arrive before taking action.†

These utterances represented fairly accurately the views of the British Government on the subject. When a statement was published in the *Standard* on 14 May that the German Government intended to take over the suzerainty of Angra Pequena, the English claim being regarded as altogether invalid, Lord Derby concluded that this report must be "entirely unfounded, as Her Majesty's Government have now under their consideration Count Münster's letter of 31st December last, a copy of which was enclosed in your letter of the 19th January. At the same time, his Lordship would be glad to know whether Lord Granville is in possession of any further information on the subject."‡ But the foreign office was at a loss. They did not think they had received any information as to the assumption of sovereignty by Germany, and, with Count Münster's note still unanswered, there was some difficulty about making inquiries at Berlin (2) . It was decided to tell Münster that an answer from the Cape was shortly expected, and at the same time the colonial office was pressed to let no delay occur in giving an answer to the German inquiries.§

* 17 May 1884. Count Münster to Prince Bismarck. German White Book, *Angra Pequena,* No. 14.

† 19 May 1884. *Hansard Parliamentary Debates,* 3rd Series, CCLXXXVIII, pp. 646-7.

‡ 17 May 1884. Colonial office to foreign office. British Blue Book, (C. 4190), No. 49.

§ 22 May 1884. Foreign office to colonial office. *Ibid.,* No. 51.

The public utterances which had been made by Lord Derby provoked a vigorous reaction from Bismarck, who now took steps to make it clear to the British Government that he considered Angra Pequena a question of primary importance. However, while he protested against the British act of referring the matter to the Cape Colony, Bismarck apparently assumed that his intentions in regard to Angra Pequena were already clear, and he did nothing to make them clearer, until the beginning of June. Thus, until the beginning of June, Granville and Derby continued to believe that Bismarck had no intention of setting up at Angra Pequena such an arrangement as would exclude the possibility of annexation by another power, and they were correspondingly slow to comply with his wishes.

Count Hatzfeldt, the German foreign secretary, suggested to Bismarck, in a memorandum of 19 May 1884, that Lord Granville be informed that Angra Pequena was one of the questions on which Germany awaited an obliging policy from England in return for German kindnesses in other fields. To this Bismarck agreed. Hatzfeldt went on to suggest that Count Münster be "very confidentially informed of our intentions so far as is necessary so that he does not underestimate the importance which we attach to this matter." Upon this Bismarck commented: "No, on no account anyone who does not *of necessity* take part." It thus appears that Münster was not kept completely informed of the German plans. Bismarck also directed that Münster should be pressed for an answer to the telegraphic instructions of 24 April 1884 (3).

On 21 May 1884 a telegram was accordingly sent to Münster, saying that the chancellor desired a report on the execution of the instructions contained in the telegram of 24 April, and on the reply which Granville had made. Münster was also requested to tell Lord Granville that this matter was one of those in which the German Government expected a return for their kindnesses in other fields (4). Münster telegraphed back on the same day that Lord Granville's reply had been that he would place himself in communication with the colonial office. Münster went on to say that since then he had brought the matter up more than once, but had always received the answer that the Cape Colony was being consulted, and the ministerial crisis there was the cause of the delay. Bismarck strongly objected to such a view of the situation. He directed that the reply should be made: "Our future attitude does not depend upon that of the colonial office but upon that of the English Government. We cannot let ourselves be put off by reference to colonial ministers and governments" (5). This message was passed on to Münster in a telegram of 24 May, which also pointed out that Derby's public utterances and his invitation to the Cape Colony to annex Angra Pequena could hardly have taken place without Lord Granville's knowledge, and asked Münster to report on the reception that had been accorded his note of 31 December 1883 at the time he submitted it (6). These instructions were followed up by a telegram on 25 May, asking Münster not to mention Heligoland any further, because of England's attitude about Angra Pequena. To bring up this question might furnish England with the excuse to put Germany's African claims on the same footing as her right to Heligoland.*

Bismarck was beginning to push the matter. On 25 May, he ordered that his telegram of 24 April 1884 to the German consul in Cape Town, announcing that Angra Pequena was under German protection, should be published (7). The German press had already taken umbrage at Lord Derby's statement to the deputation of South African merchants, and the appearance of Bismarck's telegram became the occasion for a further series of tirades against the British Government (8).

But, although Bismarck was willing to make public the steps which he had officially taken, and to arouse German national feeling by this means, he was less inclined to publish information about his plans for the future, and was especially reticent upon the question of whether or not he intended

* 25 May 1884. Prince Bismarck to Count Münster. Telegram. *Die Grosse Politik,* IV, No. 741.

to found a German colony at Angra Pequena. In August 1883, as has been related, Lüderitz was advised, through the medium of the consul in Cape Town, not to discuss the attitude of the German Government towards his projects. But the suspicions of the interested parties in the colony had been by no means quieted, and on 8 April 1884 there appeared in the *Cape Times* a letter from Captain Spence, urging the annexation of South West Africa, in view of the intentions of the Germans. Bismarck, when Hatzfeldt brought this to his notice in a memorandum dated 23 May, commented: "all further *correspondence* with Lüderitz or the Cape is undesirable; act first. Lüderitz is losing patience, and possibly provokes thereby possible steps of priority." The publication, in the Berlin *Export* of 20 May, of a rumor that Germany was going to hoist the flag over Angra Pequena, had also aroused Bismarck's annoyance, and he added, in a further marginal comment: "it is by no means yet time for utterances from which the intention to found a colony could be gathered, and the journalistic indiscretions (Export) are to be regretted; but we cannot wait longer for answers from England; they will always just refer to 'consultations' with colonial governments or with someone else, dilatorily" (9).

Before Bismarck could take any further action, two reports arrived from Münster, giving further information about the attitude of the British Government. In a despatch of 26 May 1884, Münster went to some pains to show that he had carefully executed all his instructions on the subject of Angra Pequena. In accordance with the instructions of 27 December 1883, he had delivered a note to the British Government on 31 December, but, although he had frequently brought this matter up since then with Lord Granville, Sir Julian Pauncefote, and Lord Derby, he had always received the answer that the colonial office must communicate with the Cape Government, which involved the loss of a certain amount of time. The instructions of 24 April had also been faithfully executed, and Münster had attempted to impress upon Lord Granville the importance which Bismarck attached to this matter. Lord Granville had replied he would gladly do all he could, but the matter was held up by the ministerial crisis at the Cape. Münster thought the British Government had some justification for their delay. "The handling of all colonial matters," he wrote, "is difficult here because the English Government allows the greatest independence to the colonies. The colonial secretary is therefore also more independent of his colleagues than the other ministers, is responsible to Parliament, and in both houses all questions that have reference to colonies are very rarely addressed to the representatives of the foreign office, but always to the representatives of the colonial office." Münster then went on to describe the reply which Lord Derby had made in the House of Lords on 19 May, which has already been discussed above (10).

On 27 May Münster had another conversation with Granville, this time at the latter's instigation. He was informed that an answer from the Cape was expected in a few days, and that he would then receive an answer to his note of 31 December 1883.* According to Granville, Münster made at this interview the statement that, "as far as he knew, no steps had been taken in the matter by the German Government."†

At this point we must break off the narrative for a moment to say something about one of the most-discussed incidents of Münster's mission, the despatch of 5 May 1884 and the circumstances surrounding it and resulting from it. There has been a good deal of misguided talk about this despatch. It has been alleged that Bismarck revoked the despatch shortly after it was sent so that it was never communicated to the British Government, that he then printed it in a German White Book, and that he referred to it publicly in a speech before the Reichstag, blaming the British Government for not sending him a reply.‡ As a matter of fact, the only section of

* 27 May 1884. Count Münster to Prince Bismarck. German White Book, *Angra Pequena,* No. 20.

† 27 May 1884. Lord Granville to Lord Ampthill. British Blue Book, (C. 4190), No. 53, Enclosure.

‡ 1 January 1907, Memorandum by Mr. Eyre A. Crowe; 21 February 1907,

the despatch revoked was the instructions pertaining to Heligoland, which Münster had already carried out. Furthermore, no mention of the despatch of 5 May 1884 can be found in Bismarck's speeches to the Reichstag, nor was it ever printed in a German White Book.* Indeed the only contemporary government publication which made any reference to it was a British Blue Book on New Guinea, where the despatch was partially described in a report from Sir Edward Malet, the British ambassador to Berlin, to whom Bismarck had read it aloud.† Malet's report, written in January 1885, was the first information the British Government had about the despatch of 5 May 1884, and it came as a complete surprise. This was because Münster had not carried out his instructions. Bismarck probably realized this; in any case he never, publicly or privately, blamed England for not replying; his reason for reading the despatch to Malet was, he said, to show how different had been the situation a year before. The despatch of 5 May was really less significant than subsequent discussion makes it appear. All that happened was that Bismarck, dropping Angra Pequena for the moment, suggested a more general understanding with England on oversea affairs, at the same time proposing the cession of Heligoland. Münster, failing to see Bismarck's main point and being specially interested in Heligoland, bungled the matter completely. When the Angra Pequena affair became urgent Bismarck revoked his instructions about Heligoland. The proposal for a general understanding on oversea affairs was apparently never made by Münster to the British Government, and Bismarck, while he did not revoke his instructions in this regard, never took the matter up further. From this point on

Memorandum by Lord Sanderson, with marginal comments by Mr. Crowe. G. P. Gooch and Harold Temperley: *British Documents on the Origins of the War, 1898-1914,* III, 397-420, 421-31. Cf. also: Lord Edmond Fitzmaurice: *Life of Lord Granville,* II, 427. Sir Rennell Rodd's introduction to E. T. S. Dugdale: *German Diplomatic Documents, 1871-1914,* I, vii.

* Friedrich Thimme: *Das Memorandum E. A. Crowes vom 1. Januar 1907; Das "berühmte Schwindeldokument" E. A. Crowes. Berliner Monatshefte,* VII, 732-68, 874-79.

† 24 January 1885. Sir Edward Malet to Lord Granville. British Blue Book, (C. 4273), No. 148a.

he confined himself to concrete issues such as the Fiji Islands and Angra Pequena.

Count Münster's protestations failed to convince his chief that he was carrying out his instructions with sufficient vigor. By this time, in fact, it was quite clear that Münster had missed the point of Bismarck's policy. He had made no report, at the time, on the execution of the instructions of 31 December 1883 and of 24 April 1884, and he had also allowed the Fiji question to hang fire. His slackness was severely criticized by Bismarck in a long despatch of 1 June 1884. The chancellor wrote that the reports sent by Münster late in May had strengthened in him the impression derived from the report of 8 May, that his and Münster's views of the situation in regard to England were not the same. Heligoland, he said, was mentioned in the instructions of 5 May as a matter of only secondary importance, and this fact was especially stressed in the despatch of 11 May, where Bismarck had shown that he was more anxious to learn whether England was willing, in return for Germany's continued support, to satisfy Germany's oversea claims, and not to stand in the way of the justifiable undertakings of German subjects. Münster, according to his later reports, appeared to have restricted himself to the subject of Heligoland, and Bismarck did not know whether or not he had put before Lord Granville the alternatives, either of securing Germany's support by a fair attitude towards Germany's oversea interests, or of seeing Germany seek the advancement of her interests by arrangement with other powers. There followed a long complaint over England's attitude in colonial matters, especially in regard to Angra Pequena. Why, Bismarck asked, should the right to colonize, which England practiced so fully, be forbidden to Germany? Lord Derby had treated the territory of Angra Pequena as *res nullius,* and therefore Münster would have been all the more justified in expressing his surprise that, at the interpellation of Lord Sidmouth, Lord Derby had not recognized Germany's right to trade there. If Germany really had intentions of colonizing, how could Lord Granville dispute her right to do so, when he allowed this right to the Cape Colony? Furthermore, the appeals to the independence of the colonies and the reference to the colonial office were merely evasions, and Münster should on no account have any conversations with Lord Derby on colonial matters. In addition to this, Bismarck repeated his instructions of 25 May, to say nothing further about Heligoland.*

On 27 May Viscount Sidmouth had brought up the question of Angra Pequena in the House of Lords for the third time. Bismarck's telegram of 24 April to the German consul in Cape Town had been published in *The Times* that morning, and Sidmouth wanted to know if it were true "that possession had been formally taken by the German Government, and that protection had been promised while the negotiations were pending to all German commercial residents? It did appear to him extraordinary that while negotiations were pending a document of so authoritative a nature as that bearing the signature of Prince Bismarck should have been issued." Lord Granville replied that "from the official accounts that we have received there is no reason to think that any national flag is going to be hoisted on the spot," and that the negotiations were still going on.† Münster reported this interpellation in a despatch of 28 May.‡ On 2 June a reply was sent from Berlin that Bismarck found Lord Sidmouth's question as to whether protection had been promised "somewhat surprising. For a special promise was not necessary, in order to grant protection to our citizens. The protection by the German Government of citizens of the empire was a matter of course" (11). This statement well illustrates the ambiguity of the word "protection." It is here, obviously, used in its old sense to denote something granted regularly to all German traders and not connoting annexation at all. The explana-

* 1 June 1884. Prince Bismarck to Count Münster. *Die Grosse Politik,* IV, No. 743.

† 27 May 1884. *Hansard Parliamentary Debates,* CCLXXXVIII, pp. 1449-1450.

‡ 28 May 1884. Count Münster to Prince Bismarck. No. 75. Reichsarchiv, Vermischtes Südwestafrika III.

tion from Berlin probably only served to increase Münster's misconception.

A new element was now introduced into the negotiations, when the Cape Government, after long hesitation, suddenly made up their minds to annex Angra Pequena. On 29 May 1884, the governor of the colony telegraphed to London that the ministers had decided "to recommend Parliament to undertake control and cost of coast line from Orange River to Walfisch Bay."* On the basis of this telegram, Lord Derby suggested to the foreign office on 2 June, "that the German Government be informed that after careful consideration, and communication with the Government of the Cape Colony, Her Majesty's Government have decided that arrangements shall be made for giving protection under the British flag to any persons, German as well as English, who may have duly acquired concessions, or established commercial enterprises, on the coast between these two points. . . ."† No immediate action was taken, however, on the suggestions of the colonial office. Sir George Dallas, who appears to have seen things more clearly at this time than anyone else in the foreign office, pointed out that one of Count Münster's questions, as to the title upon which the claim of British sovereignty was based, was still unanswered. But Sir Julian Pauncefote saw no objection to the course which the colonial office had proposed. He wrote: "The G.G. have asked what rights we claim over the territory in question, as they do not at present recognize our sovereignty and therefore must protect the German Subjects settled there. The C.O. now propose to reply that H.M.G. have decided to annex the territory as part of the British Dominions and to exercise the rights of Sovereignty thereover and consequently to extend British protection to all persons residing therein" (12). Lord Granville wrote that he must speak to Derby on the subject, and, in view of later developments, action appears to have been suspended.

* 29 May 1884. Sir Hercules Robinson to Lord Derby. Telegram. British Blue Book, (C. 4190), No. 54.

† 2 June 1884. Colonial office to foreign office. British Blue Book, (C. 4190), No. 55.

The minute of Sir Julian Pauncefote here quoted, which was written on 4 June 1884, indicates that some persons in the British Government still thought that Germany was willing to be relieved, by a British annexation, from the duty of protecting the settlement at Angra Pequena. They were soon to be disillusioned.

The prime minister of the Cape Colony had privately informed the German consul of the communication he was making to the colonial office in London, that the colony was ready to take over the coast of South West Africa up to Walfisch Bay and including Angra Pequena. This news was sent on to Berlin in a telegram of 3 June.* Bismarck immediately instructed Münster to inform Lord Granville confidentially that Germany could not recognize such an annexation, and disputed the right thereto.† This communication made a strong impression on the British Government. Granville told Münster that he would make every effort to come to a solution, but that, since the other ministers were out of London, he could not give a further answer for several days. He begged that Germany would take no action until both governments had come to an understanding. Münster reported Lord Granville's answer in a despatch of 7 June, and, no doubt stimulated by Bismarck's criticism, added that he had told Granville with the greatest emphasis what importance Bismarck attached to this matter, and how German policy could be influenced by it (13). Granville's account of the conversation, however, says nothing of the possibility of a reversal of German policy if Bismarck were dissatisfied with the British attitude on the matter in question,‡ so there is some doubt as to how effectual Count Münster's representations actually were.

On 7 June Lord Granville had a further conversation with Count Münster on the same subject. Münster found Gran-

* 3 June 1884. Lippert, the German consul in Cape Town, to the German foreign office. Telegram. German White Book, *Angra Pequena,* No. 21.

† 4 June 1884. Count Hatzfeldt to Count Münster. Telegram. *Ibid.,* No. 22.

‡ 7 June 1884. Lord Granville to Lord Ampthill. British Blue Book, (C. 4190), No. 62, Enclosure.

ville "much worried and upset" by the latest German communication. "I am taken aback by your Government's abrupt action," said Lord Granville. He brought forward the old excuses for delay, the consultation with the Cape Colony and the ministerial crisis there, and complained that Germany had taken action before a settlement had been achieved. "Neither my colleagues nor myself," he said, "have the slightest intention of obstructing German Colonial aspirations, and I beg you to say so plainly to Prince Bismarck. I must, however, observe that I have not formed the impression from any of the communications which have passed between Count Bismarck and myself, or between the Chancellor and Lord Ampthill, that the German Government wish to pursue a Colonial policy."* These words have the appearance of sincerity. The theory that the British Government realized Bismarck's intentions at an early stage of the proceedings, and tried to anticipate him by a *fait accompli,* is untenable. The fact that Münster did not, until June 1884, realize that Bismarck was intent upon a colonial policy, is alone sufficient to disprove such a charge. That the German decision to take control of Angra Pequena came as a complete surprise to the British Government is shown by Lord Derby's minute of 8 June upon the German communication of 4 June: "This seems to mean that the German Government intends to lay claim to Angra Pequena as German territory. Of course they do not mean to include Walfish [sic] Bay, which we have held since 1877 or 78,—they not objecting. We must abstain from taking any action on the recommendation of the Cape colony, till the question of right is settled. . . . Our claim may not be a strong one, I do not think it is; but I cannot conceive what claim the Germans have to put forward."†

Not until now did Bismarck take the matter up with Lord Ampthill. As has already been shown, the British ambassador did not realize until extremely late the turn events were tak-

* 7 June 1884. Count Münster to Prince Bismarck. *Die Grosse Politik,* IV, No. 744. The passages quoted are taken from the translation of E. T. S. Dugdale: *German Diplomatic Documents, 1871-1914,* I, 177–78.

† 8 June 1884. Minute by Lord Derby. Private Granville MSS, G.D. 29/180.

ing, and his most recent communications had served only to aggravate the misunderstanding of the British Government. The report in the *Standard* of 14 May, that Germany was taking over the suzerainty of Angra Pequena, was sent to him on the 22nd.* Lord Ampthill replied categorically that "the report in the 'Standard' of May 14th respecting the alleged assumption of the sovereignty of that territory by the German Government is unfounded." The rumor was due, he said, to the growing impatience of the German people for a colonial policy.† Until June 1884, Bismarck had not discussed Angra Pequena with Lord Ampthill at all, although, at the beginning of April 1884, he had alluded to "important German interests on the West Coast of Africa and on the Congo, which the great Commercial Communities of Bremen and Hamburgh [sic] were pressing him to protect" (14). But the ambassador received no more definite intimation from the German foreign office about Angra Pequena, until Count Hatzfeldt brought up the subject on 6 June 1884. Hatzfeldt then said that "Prince Bismarck had given orders that the confidential communication made by the Premier at Capetown to the German Consul should be kept secret, so as to avoid the painful impression it would produce on Public opinion in Germany, until an answer had been received from your Lordship through Count Münster." But Bismarck would soon have to answer questions about Angra Pequena in the Reichstag, and would be grateful if the British Government would answer Count Münster's note of 31 December 1883, and thus put him in the position to give a satisfactory explanation. In reply, Ampthill reminded Count Hatzfeldt of Derby's explanation in the House of Lords, and of the correspondence which had passed between Granville and Münster so far as he was familiar with it himself, but he found that Count Hatzfeldt "looked upon the assumption of the Right of Sovereignty over Angra Pequena by the Cape Government

* 22 May 1884. British foreign office to Lord Ampthill. No. 142. Draft. F.O. 64/1102.

† 30 May 1884. Lord Ampthill to Lord Granville. British Blue Book, (C. 4190), No. 58, Enclosure 1.

in the light of a surprise for which the German Government was quite unprepared."* "My impression is," wrote Hatzfeldt, in his account of the conversation, "that he [Lord Ampthill] keenly regrets the incident, and will strongly urge a change of policy in London" (15).

Lord Ampthill's despatch describing this conversation, when it arrived in London on 9 June, quickened the suspicion which was already present there that the German designs had not been completely understood. Dallas suggested that, in the circumstances described by Ampthill, the answer proposed by the colonial office in their letter of 2 June would hardly be very palatable to the German Government. Pauncefote thought, however, that a note had better be drafted along the lines proposed by the colonial office, for consideration (16). But, in view of further developments, action was again suspended.

On 7 June Lord Ampthill sent a further despatch, reporting a resolution unanimously adopted at a general meeting of the West German Society for Colonization and Export Trade at Düsseldorf on 5 June. This resolution expressed the society's grateful satisfaction at "the recent preparatory steps taken by the Imperial Government to protect Germany's present and future interest in the district of the Congo, and on the West Coast of Central Africa." The society was gratified by the declaration that Angra Pequena had been placed under German protection, and expressed a confident hope that German protection might also be extended to the more northerly coast line of Hereroland, "not only in consideration of the German interests which have existed there for many years past, but also in order to secure a sufficient working basis for German enterprises on the coast of South Africa."† Again, Sir George Dallas saw rather further than his colleagues, when he commented on this despatch: "It seems to become a question now what the German Gt. meant by

* 6 June 1884, (Received 9 June). Lord Ampthill to Lord Granville. No. 143. Confidential. F.O. 64/1102.

† 7 June 1884. Lord Ampthill to Lord Granville. British Blue Book, (C. 4190), No. 59, Enclosure.

intimating that Angra Pequena had been placed under the protection of the Empire. Do they intend to claim sovereignty over the place?" Pauncefote rejoined: "I think not. Their language has been that as we do not claim sovereignty, German subjects are entitled to German protection. But they may lately have some scheme of a German Protectorate there." Lord Granville was disposed to be cautious. "We had better wait till we see H. Bismarck," he wrote.* (Count Herbert Bismarck, the chancellor's son, was expected to arrive in London within a few days.)

Probably Granville's eyes had been partially opened by the receipt of a private letter from Lord Ampthill, also of 7 June. In this letter, the ambassador pointed out the seriousness of the colonial agitation in Germany, and the probability of "a phase of ill humour on the part of Prince Bismarck if we are unable to meet his wishes in colonial questions and give him the means at the Eve of a general Election of effectually calming down the growing storm of indignation against himself and us, for standing between the German Colonial Party and the distant objects of their passionate desire!" As Bismarck was soon to return to Berlin, and might bring the matter up in conversation, Ampthill begged to be informed, if possible by telegram, what answer had been made to Count Münster (17).

The communication which Münster had been instructed to make on 4 June 1884, together with the altered tone of the despatches from Lord Ampthill, had succeeded in giving the British Government some intimation of Bismarck's real intentions in regard to Angra Pequena, which Münster, in the whole period following his return to London at the end of April, had failed to do. There can be no doubt that in his conduct of the negotiations the German ambassador had made a number of very serious mistakes. In his enthusiasm for the project of Heligoland, he had ignored Bismarck's desire, expressed in the despatch of 5 May, for a general understanding with England in regard to oversea questions. He did not

* Three undated minutes by Sir George Dallas, Sir Julian Pauncefote and Lord Granville upon Lord Ampthill's despatch of 7 June 1884. F.O. 64/1102.

point out to Granville the possibility of a reversal of German policy in Egypt until after he had been severely reprimanded in the despatch of 1 June, and even then he did not do it effectively. As for Angra Pequena, he did not make clear Bismarck's great point that Germany could deal only with the British Government, and not with the colonial office or the Cape Colony. On the contrary, he appears to have sympathized with the British Government in their difficulties, and even to have made excuses for them in his despatches to Berlin. According to a statement made by Count Herbert Bismarck, Münster even went so far as to invite England to extend her protection to Angra Pequena.* This charge is at any rate *ben trovato*.

The chief reason for Münster's extraordinary conduct was that he entirely failed to realize Bismarck's intention of founding a colony at Angra Pequena. It was this fact that induced him not to press the question of Angra Pequena more strongly, and even lured him into what was in effect disobedience of his instructions. His attitude is clearly shown in a despatch of 6 June, in which he attempted to justify the attitude of the British Government, and to show that he had executed his instructions in the manner desired. He began his discussion of Angra Pequena by quoting the instructions to Count Herbert Bismarck of 4 February 1883, in which it had been stated that Germany was not interested in oversea projects. "The explanation," he wrote, "which Count Herbert Bismarck gave at the beginning of the negotiations over Angra Pequena has not been without influence on the policy and the views of the British Government. . . . Lord Granville and Lord Derby are still under the impression that the Imperial Government on no account *wishes* to found a German colony at Angra Pequena. Our right to found colonies has been disputed, so far as I know, by neither of them." A little later in the despatch, he added: "As far as concerns my personal attitude towards the German colonial

* 24 June 1884. Letter from Count Herbert Bismarck in London. Hans Rothfels: *Bismarcks Englische Bündnispolitik,* p. 82, footnote 1.

attempts . . . I have always believed that I stood in the same position as Your Serene Highness. The above-quoted passage from the instructions of 4 February of last year, 'that now, as formerly, we have no thought of any oversea projects,' had strengthened me in this belief" (18).

There was another factor in Münster's conduct that must on no account be disregarded, his personal character. There would seem to be more than a germ of truth in the remark of Bucher, Bismarck's secretary, that Münster was "more English than German."* The ambassador was a Hanoverian, and his father is reported to have represented Hanover in London when his country was still under the sovereignty of the king of England. Münster had been educated in England, spoke the language well and had married an English wife.† In spite of his liking for English customs he was, Granville wrote, "very unpopular with the Royalties here. They object to him as a Hanoverian renegade and he is not remarkable for tact."‡ In Berlin Münster was regarded as "an advanced Liberal suffering from Anglomania."§ Ampthill reported that "Münster is out of favour with Bismarck because he thinks him too English and too liberal."|| In the colonial negotiations it is apparent that Münster was always ready to appreciate the English point of view and expound it to his chief, and as late as February 1885 we again find him laboriously explaining to Bismarck the very argument that Bismarck had continually told him to protest against, that English foreign policy must of necessity be conducted with reference to the colonies (19).

Not only was Münster somewhat inclined to the English side, but Bismarck's opinion of him was never a high one in any case. Lord Ampthill tells a story that the "Prince of

* M. Busch: *Bismarck, Some Secret Pages of His History,* III, 118.

† Graf von Beust: *Aus Drei Viertel-Jahrhunderten,* II, 546.

‡ 4 May 1881. Lord Granville to Lord Ampthill. Draft. Private Granville MSS, G.D. 29/206.

§ 18 November 1882. Lord Ampthill to Lord Granville. Private Granville MSS, G.D. 29/178.

|| 18 April 1881. Lord Ampthill to Lord Granville. Private and Personal. Private Granville MSS, G.D. 29/177.

Wales and Princess Christian* during their recent stay at Berlin exerted all their influence to get Count Münster recalled and General von Schweinitz appointed to London. The Crown Prince and Princess, who have hitherto protected Münster have had their faith in him shaken thereby, and have broached the subject with Bismarck, who replied that he had appointed Münster to please their Imp. and Royal Highness's and that he should remain in London just as long or just as little as they pleased." Ampthill added, however, that he did not anticipate a change at the moment.† In addition to this, Münster seems to have been jealous of Herbert, Bismarck's favorite son and his subordinate in London, and to have unburdened himself indiscreetly to the Crown Prince and Princess. Lord Ampthill reported: "Münster's language at Berlin about Herbert was almost as bad as his dinners in London,–and if the Chancellor gets wind of the imprudent criticisms uttered at Potsdam to gratify their Imperial Highness's objections to all the Bismarck family, Münster will be made to rue it in retirement at Derneburg some fine morning."‡ Two years later Dilke found Münster "very free in his remarks about Bismarck."§ If Münster was in the habit of making such confidences it is not unlikely that word of them did reach the chancellor in time, and reacted on him as one might expect.

There is no excuse for Münster's neglect of his more specific instructions, but it is easy to understand how he failed to appreciate the general trend of the Angra Pequena negotiations. The instructions of 4 February 1883 had been very misleading, and had never been contradicted. Bismarck, feeling as he did about Münster, was hardly likely to take him much into his confidence, and, when Hatzfeldt suggested in

* This was Princess Helena, daughter of Queen Victoria of England, who married Prince Frederick Christian of Schleswig-Holstein-Sonderburg-Augustenburg.

† 18 April 1881. Lord Ampthill to Lord Granville. Private and Personal. Private Granville MSS, G.D. 29/177.

‡ 18 November 1882. Lord Ampthill to Lord Granville. Private Granville MSS, G.D. 29/178.

§ Gwynn and Tuckwell: *Life of Sir Charles W. Dilke,* II, 99.

COUNT MÜNSTER

May 1884 that Münster be further informed of the German intentions, Bismarck emphatically rejected the proposal. Furthermore, Bismarck had not yet stated, either to the ambassador or to anyone else, his intention of founding a colony at Angra Pequena. Even during June and July 1884, Bismarck's language was that he did not intend to found a colony in the accepted sense of the word, but to exercise a sort of protection over the territory acquired by German traders, who would be given a "royal charter" drawn up on the English model. But the term "protection" had been used by the German Government in the past to signify assistance from the nearest German consul and, occasionally, from a German warship as well, which was a very different thing. This type of protection had been granted to German traders for many years past; it was the type which it was originally proposed to grant to Lüderitz, and the official announcement of 24 April 1884 was not accompanied by any definition of the new meaning attached to this ambiguous word. In these circumstances it is hardly surprising that Münster, like everyone else, failed to realize what Bismarck had in his mind.

NOTES

1. 1 May 1884. Lüderitz to Prince Bismarck. Reichsarchiv. Vermischtes Südwestafrika II.

". . . Ich gehe dabei von der Voraussetzung aus, dass es keine Reichskolonie unter Kaiserlich deutscher Verwaltung werden soll, sondern dass ich (bzw. eine von mir zu bildende Gesellschaft) die nöthigen Verwaltungsbeamten selbst anstellen und besolden werde." (Bismarck: "ja.")

2. Three undated minutes by Sir George Dallas, Sir Philip Currie, and Lord Granville, on the letter from the colonial office to the foreign office of 17 May 1884. F.O. 64/1102.

"We have no information as to the assumption of Sovereignty by Germany. There would be a certain difficulty about making inquiries at Berlin as we have not yet answered Ct. Münster's commn. of December last, but we might perhaps send the Col. Office letter to Ld. Ampthill for his observations, and inform the Col. Office.

"G. Dl.

"or perhaps Lord Granville will tell Ct. Münster that the Colonial Office are expecting a definite reply from the Cape Govt. in the course of a few days (See telegram from Sir H. Robinson).

"P. C.

"I concur. Remind me at my next interview with Munster. Press Col. Office to let no unnecessary delay occur.

"G."

3. 19 May 1884. Memorandum by Count Hatzfeldt on Angra Pequena. Seen by Bismarck on 21 May. Reichsarchiv, Vermischtes Südwestafrika III.

"Bei Vorlegung des Berichts aus London vom 13. d.M. . . . und des Berichts vom 17. d.M. . . . , betreffend Angra Pequena, bitte ich Euere Durchlaucht um geneigte Bestimmung, ob Lord Granville darauf aufmerksam gemacht werden soll, dass diese Frage zu denjenigen gehört, bei welchen wir ein Entgegenkommen Englands in Erwiderung unserer Gefälligkeiten auf anderen Gebieten erwarten. Denn bei den jüngst in letzterer Hinsicht nach London gerichteten Erlassen war Angra Pequena nicht besonders erwähnt worden. (Bismarck: ja.)

"Zugleich würde Graf Münster vielleicht ganz vertraulich soweit von unseren Absichten zu informiren sein, als erforderlich ist, damit er den Werth, den wir auf diese Angelegenheit legen, nicht unterschätzt. (Bismarck: nein, keinenfalls irgend jemand der nicht *nothwendig* mitwirkt.)

"Dies erscheint um so rathsamer, als er das gehorsamst wieder beigefügte Telegramm Euerer Durchlaucht vom 24. v.M., No. 20, bisher nicht beantwortet hat. (Bismarck: Graf Münster ist sofort um Antwort zu excitiren.)"

4. 21 May 1884. Count Hatzfeldt to Count Münster. Cipher telegram. No. 28. Reichsarchiv, Vermischtes Südwestafrika III. (An incomplete summary of this telegram appears in German White Book, *Angra Pequena,* No. 15.)

"Der Herr Reichskanzler vermisst eine Anzeige wann und wie Ew. pp. sein Telegramm No. 20 vom 24. v.M., betreffend Angra Pequena, erledigt haben, und was Lord Granville auf Ihre Mittheilung geantwortet hat.

"Fürst Bismarck wünscht, dass Ew. pp. Lord Granville besonders aufmerksam machen, dass diese Angelegenheit zu denjenigen gehört, in welchen wir eine Erwiderung der auf anderen Gebieten von uns beanspruchten Gefälligkeiten erwarten."

5. 21 May 1884. Count Münster to German foreign office. Cipher telegram. No. 59. Reichsarchiv, Vermischtes Südwestafrika III. An accurate summary of this telegram appears in German White Book, *Angra Pequena,* No. 16. Bismarck's marginal comment is as follows:

"resp.: unsre künftige Haltung hänge nicht von der des Colonial-Amtes sondern von der der engl. Regierung ab. Wir können uns mit Berufung auf Colonial-Minister und Regierungen nicht abspeisen lassen."

6. 24 May 1884. Count Hatzfeldt to Count Münster. Cipher telegram. No. 29. Reichsarchiv, Vermischtes Südwestafrika III. (Part of this telegram is given in the German White Book, *Angra Pequena,* No. 17.)

"Zu Ew. (tit.) Telegram No. 59 bemerkt der Herr Reichskanzler, dass unsere künftige Haltung hänge nicht von der des Colonial-Amts sondern von der der englischen Regierung ab. Wir können uns mit Berufung auf Colonial-Minister und Regierungen nicht abspeisen lassen.

"Die Aeusserungen Lord Derby's gegenüber der Deputation und im Parlament und seine an die Kap-Regierung telegraphisch gerichteten indirekten Ermunterungen zur nachträglichen Annexion von Angra Pequena können kaum ohne Vorwissen Lord Granville's erfolgt sein.

"Um so wichtiger für unsere Beurtheilung wäre daher der noch fehlende Bericht mit genauen Daten über Erledigung des Erlasses vom 27. December v. Js. und über die Aufnahme, welche Ihre Note und deren mündliche Ergänzungen damals gefunden haben."

7. 25 May 1884. Prince Bismarck to German foreign office. Cipher telegram. No. 2. Reichsarchiv, Vermischtes Südwestafrika III.

"Ich bitte unser wegen Angra Pequena die Regierung von Kapland an dortigen Konsul gerichtetes Telegramm ohne weiteren Kommentar als die einleitende Bemerkung 'dass es zur Richtigstellung der verschiedenen Nachrichten der Zeitungen dient' und den Schluss 'Weiteres liegt bisher in dieser Angelegenheit nicht vor' zu veröffentlichen."

8. The publication of Bismarck's telegram of 24 April 1884 is reported in *The Times* of 27 May 1884, p. 5, col. 2. Their correspondent quotes from the Conservative *Reichsbote* of 26 May as follows:

"We are firmly convinced that the German Government will look after legitimate German interests in their full extent on the other side of the sea. But at least it will never allow itself to be influenced by the bravado of such impotent and unprincipled statesmen as now conduct affairs in England. We must, however, characterize it as a national affront, that an English Colonial Minister should dare to forbid us from colonizing ownerless land. Surely the insulted national feeling of Germany will rouse itself, and clearly express to the English nation its displeasure at these narrow-hearted and jealous measures, which are plainly stamped with a hostile character."

This, wrote the Berlin correspondent of *The Times,* "may be taken as a fair specimen of the Chauvinistic rodomontade towards England, in which a large portion of the German Press has lately seen fit to indulge."

9. 23 May 1884. Memorandum by Count Hatzfeldt on Angra Pequena. Reichsarchiv, Vermischtes Südwestafrika III.

Count Hatzfeldt describes a letter from Mr. Spence in the *Cape Times* of 8 May, "in welcher die Annexion des ganzen Küstenstrichs bis zur Portugiesischen Grenze unter Hinweis auf dessen bedeutenden Werth und auf die Absicht der Deutschen empfohlen wird. (Bismarck: jede weitere *Correspondenz* mit Lüderitz oder mit Cap ist bedenklich; erst handeln. Lüderitz verliert die Ruhe, und provocirt dadurch möglicher Weise mögliche Prioritätsschritte.)

" . . . Was den Antrag des Agenten des Herrn Lüderitz anbelangt, . . . so empfiehlt es sich wohl, die Entschliessung hierüber bis zum Eingang der Antwort des Grafen Münster auf dasjenige Telegramm auszusetzen, durch welches ich ihn am 21. d.Mts. im Auftrage Euerer Durchlaucht zu der vermissten Aeusserung über Erledigung des Telegramms vom 24. v.Mts. ersucht habe." (Bismarck: "es ist für Äusserungen aus denen auf die Absicht eine Colonie zu gründen geschlossen werden könnte, überhaupt noch nicht Zeit und sind die publicistischen Indiscretionen (Export) zu bedauern; auf Antworten von England können wir aber weiter nicht warten; sie werden immer nur auf 'Rückfragen' bei Colonial-Regierungen oder bei sonst jemand Bezug nehmen, dilatorisch. Das Tel. vom 21. *ist* schon beantwortet?")

10. 26 May 1884. Count Münster to Prince Bismarck. No. 71. Reichsarchiv, Vermischtes Südwestafrika III. This despatch also appears in German White Book, *Angra Pequena,* No. 19, but several passages are omitted, of which the following are of importance:

"Von Seiten der Kaiserlichen Botschaft ist in dieser Angelegenheit durchaus nichts versäumt worden, und hat es auch an mündlicher Anregung von meiner Seite nicht gefehlt.

"Der hohe Erlass vom 27sten. December 1883 ist am 30sten. December hier präsentirt, und schon am anderen Tage, den 31sten., ist die Note ganz in der vorgeschriebenen Form an das hiesige Foreign Office gerichtet worden. Bis jetzt ist, trotz wiederholter Anregung, noch keine Antwort auf diese Note erfolgt, ich werde aber jetzt wieder auf deren Beantwortung dringen.

" . . . Darauf ist erst wieder am 24sten. April das Telegramm No. 20 an die hiesige Botschaft gerichtet, und der Geschäftsträger Graf Vitzthum hat am 25sten. den Auftrag Lord Granville gegenüber ausgeführt und hat die

Antwort erhalten, dass Lord Granville die Mittheilung sogleich an das Colonial-Amt gelangen lassen werde.

" . . . Die Behandlung aller Colonial-Angelegenheiten ist hier schwierig weil Seitens der Englischen Regierung den Colonien die grösste Selbständigkeit gelassen wird. (Bismarck: wir kennen nur *Eine* Regierung in England und seinen Colonien.) Der Colonial-Minister ist deshalb auch seinen Collegen gegenüber unabhängiger, als die übrigen Minister, ist dem Parlamente gegenüber verantwortlich, und alle Anfragen, die sich auf Colonien beziehen, werden in beiden Häusern höchst selten an die Vertreter des Auswärtigen, sondern stets an die des Colonial-Amts gerichtet."

11. 2 June 1884. Instructions to Münster. Draft. Reichsarchiv, Vermischtes Südwestafrika III.

"Ew. pp. gef. Bericht No. 75 vom 28. v.Mts. betreffend Angra Pequena hat dem Herrn Reichskanzler vorgelegen.

"S. D. hat dazu bemerkt, dass ihm die Frage in der Interpellation Lord Sidmouth's, ob es wahr sei 'that protection had been promised,' einigermassen befremdlich erschiene. Denn ein besonderes Versprechen sei gar nicht erforderlich gewesen, um unseren Landsleute Schutz zu gewähren. Die Protektion der Reichsangehöriger durch die deutsche Regierung sei selbstverständlich. . . . "

12. Three minutes by Sir George Dallas, Sir Julian Pauncefote, and Lord Granville, upon the letter from the colonial office to the foreign office of 2 June. Pauncefote's minute is dated 4 June 1884, the other two minutes are undated. F.O. 64/1102.

"Ct. Münster asked two questions: 1. Upon what title the claim of British Sovereignty was based. 2. What means Gt. Britain possessed of excercising in those regions the rights and duties of Sovereignty. The first question is still unanswered by the Colonial Office. Sir J. Pauncefote should see this letter at once.

"G. Dl."

The relevant part of Sir Julian Pauncefote's minute has been quoted in the text.

"I must speak to Derby on this.

"G."

13. 7 June 1884. Count Münster to German foreign office. Cipher telegram. No. 67. Reichsarchiv, Vermischtes Südwestafrika III. (There is an incomplete summary of this telegram in German White Book, *Angra Pequena,* No. 23.)

"Lord Granville, dem ich den Inhalt des Telegramms No. 33 mittheilte, erwiederte, dass ich Euerer Durchlaucht sagen möge, wie sehr er bestrebt sein werde, die entstandene Differenz auszugleichen.

"Er könne mir erst weitere Antwort Anfangs der Woche geben, da die anderen Minister noch abwesend seien. Er bedauere, dass die Antwort auf meine Note wegen des Ministerwechsels am Cap noch immer nicht erfolgt sei.

"Er bitte aber dringend, dass keine Action erfolgen möge, bis beide Regierungen zu einer Verständigung gelangt seien.

"Ich habe Lord Granville auf das bestimmteste gesagt, welchen Werth Euere Durchlaucht dieser Angelegenheit beimessen und wie die Deutsche Politik dadurch beeinflusst werden könne."

14. 13 April 1884. Lord Ampthill to Lord Granville. Private. Private Granville MSS, G.D. 29/178.

" . . . He [i.e., Bismarck] said that he had always had implicit faith in the equitable spirit of Her Majesty's Government in dealing with foreign claims,—but that he now received many complaints of the prevalence of a less equitable spirit in our Colonial Authorities,—complaints he would not be able to disregard since they involved great and growing interests of vast importance to Germany and for the equitable adjustment of which he reckoned on your assistance. Prince Bismarck also alluded to important German interests on the West Coast of Africa and on the Congo, which the great Commercial Communities of Bremen and Hamburgh [sic] were pressing him to protect and which might require the friendly coöperation, he valued so highly, of her Majesty's Government.

"Prince Bismarck's civil tone and manner sounded to me rather like a warning that he is about to ask us for more than we can grant."

15. 6 June 1884. Memorandum by Count Hatzfeldt. Reichsarchiv, Vermischtes Südwestafrika III.

"Ich habe Lord Ampthill die entspr. Eröffnung gemacht, auch in der Unterhaltung, die sich daran knüpfte, den Hergang der ganzen Sache recapitulirt. Mein Eindruck ist dass er den Zwischenfall lebhaft beklagt und in London dringend zum Einlenken rathen wird. . . . "

16. Two minutes by Sir George Dallas and Sir Julian Pauncefote on a despatch from Lord Ampthill, No 143, of 6 June 1884. F.O. 64/1102.

"Under these circs. the answer suggested by the Col. Office in their letter of June 2 (now before Ld. Granville) will hardly be very palatable to the German Govt. Sir J. Pauncefote.

"Dl.

"I think we had better draft a note as proposed in C.O. of 2 June for conson.

"J.P. 10/6/84."

17. 7 June 1884. Lord Ampthill to Lord Granville. Private. Private Granville MSS, G.D. 29/178.

"As I have said on previous occasions we must expect a phase of illhumour on the part of Prince Bismarck if we are unable to meet his wishes in colonial questions and give him the means at the Eve of a general Election of effectually calming down the growing storm of indignation against himself and us, for standing between the German Colonial Party and the distant objects of their passionate desire!

"The agitation is becoming a very serious one, and will have great influence on the coming Elections next autumn, so that Bismarck must adopt a popular and national attitude to secure a majority in the new Parliament.

" . . . I shall be glad to know what you have answered Münster about Angra Pequena, as Bismarck may speak to me about it when he comes to town.

"I should be very much obliged for a telegram."

18. 6 June 1884. Count Münster to Prince Bismarck. No. 83. Copy. Reichsarchiv, Vermischtes Südwestafrika III.

" . . . Die Erklärung, welche der Graf Herbert Bismarck bei Beginn der Verhandlungen über Angra Pequena gegeben hat, ist für die Behandlung und Anschauungsweise der Englischen Regierung nicht ohne Einfluss geblieben. . . . Lord Granville und Lord Derby sind noch jetzt unter dem Eindruck, dass die Kaiserliche Regierung eine deutsche Kolonie in Angra Pequena garnicht gründen *will*. Unser Recht Kolonien einzurichten hat meines Wissens keiner von Beiden bestritten. Dass Lord Granville mich neuerdings wieder gebeten hat, Euerer Durchlaucht zu melden, dass er auch speciell in der Angra-Pequena-Angelegenheit Alles thun werde, um eine

Verständigung mit der Kaiserlichen Regierung herbeizuführen, habe ich in meinem Bericht vom 27. v.Mts.—No. 72—bereits zu Eurer Durchlaucht Kenntniss gebracht.

" . . . Was meine persönliche Stellung zu den deutschen Kolonisationsbestrebungen betrifft, auf welche Eure Durchlaucht in dem hohen Erlass Bezug nehmen, so habe ich immer geglaubt, auf demselben Standpunkt wie Euere Durchlaucht zu stehen. Der obenangeführte Passus des Erlasses vom 4. Februar v. J's. 'dass uns jetzt wie früher alle überseeischen Projekte fernlägen' hatte mich in diesem Glauben bestärkt."

19. 4 February 1885. Count Münster to Prince Bismarck. No. 17. Reichsarchiv, Vermischtes Neu-Guinea XII.

" . . . Mr. Gladstone und seine Anhänger haben die Kolonien stets sehr schlecht behandelt und haben nicht den Werth auf sie gelegt, den sie für England haben. In der liberalen Partei selbst ist das erkannt und es bildet sich jetzt eine Partei, an deren Spitze Lord Rosebery und Mr. Foster stehen, welche sogenannte Imperial Policy treiben und die Idee haben, den Kolonien hier eine bessere und wirksamere Vertretung zu verschaffen. (Bismarck: immer Frage für England.)

"Eine Verstimmung Australiens würde gerade diese Bestrebungen sehr hemmen. Bei den jüngeren radikalen Politikern hat die Imperial Policy viele Anhänger. Die letzten Vorgänge in Neu-Guinea sind auf übertriebene Rücksichtnahme gegen Australien zurückzuführen. (Bismarck: wirklich!) . . . "

V

COUNT HERBERT BISMARCK'S MISSION

ALTHOUGH, in the first week of June 1884, Count Münster's representations became more vigorous, he did not point out with the emphasis Bismarck desired the possibility of a reversal of German policy in Egypt, if Germany were not satisfied in colonial questions, and he entirely failed to make clear, or even to appreciate, Bismarck's wish to take over Angra Pequena himself. The British foreign office failed to realize that Germany intended to assert an exclusive claim to Angra Pequena, and, early in June, even went so far as to draft a note to Count Münster, answering his note of 31 December 1883, and informing him that the British Government had decided that "arrangements shall be made for giving protection under the British flag to any persons, German as well as English, who may have duly acquired concessions, or established commercial enterprises, on that portion of the coast of Africa, which lies between the Orange River and Walwich [sic] Bay" (1).

But Münster's communication of 4 June 1884, that the German Government could not recognize such an annexation of the coast of South West Africa as had been suggested by the Cape Colony, had put the British Government on their guard, and the altered tone in the despatches of Lord Ampthill had also aroused their suspicions. On 10 June 1884 Lord Granville telegraphed to Ampthill: "I hope to have a full discussion with Herbert Bismarck on Angra Pequena question."* Count Herbert Bismarck was daily expected in London, and Lord Granville decided to wait for him before

*10 June 1884. Lord Granville to Lord Ampthill. Cipher telegram. Private. Private Granville MSS, G.D. 29/206.

taking any action (2). Thus, fortunately for the good relations between Germany and England, the note to Count Münster which had been drafted was never sent.

But the long duration of the negotiations had attracted attention in England, and when Viscount Sidmouth brought up the matter again, in the House of Lords on 13 June 1884, the Earl of Carnarvon added his protest also. The subject was a serious one, he said, and it was "still more serious that the negotiations should be allowed to drag on for such a great length of time, as in that part of the world the British and the German interests touched each other very closely." It had always been his experience that German policy was conducted in a reasonable spirit, and he would be glad to see the question disposed of satisfactorily and without delay.*

Apparently Bismarck was also troubled by the way in which this question had been held up, for on 10 June 1884 he wrote a long despatch to Münster, recapitulating the negotiations and complaining that England had not treated Germany fairly. He had tried to ascertain England's rights over Angra Pequena "without unnecessarily awakening fears about our intentions or the desire to anticipate them." For this reason, he had put his question in the form of whether England was in a position to grant protection to German settlements in South Africa. Although he already knew that this was not the case, he had desired an official statement from the British Government. His question as to England's claims and title could have been answered in a week, without reference to the Cape Government. An examination of the list of English annexations would have sufficed. But this simple question had been interpreted by Lord Derby and Lord Granville to mean that Germany had asked whether England would perhaps like to annex something else besides Walfisch Bay on that coast. The claim that the vicinity of English possessions gave England the right to exclude other powers from the territory in question was grossly unfair, and Bismarck thought England had not treated Germany with justice. He had, he said, dis-

* 13 June 1884. *Hansard Parliamentary Debates,* CCLXXXIX, 237-38.

cussed this question with Lord Ampthill the day before, and had explained to him that Germany could not refuse protection to her citizens when it was demanded. Bismarck added that he did not intend to establish a colonial system like the English one, "with garrisons, governors, and officials," but was thinking of something along the lines of the English East India Company. He asked Münster to gather from this despatch the line he should take with Lord Granville, and said that it was essential to avoid making the impression of having sacrificed the vital interests of Germany to a good understanding with England, however desirable that might be in itself.*

Münster did not have an opportunity to act on these instructions, for, on 14 June 1884, the negotiations were taken out of his hands by Count Herbert Bismarck, who, having been appointed German minister to the Hague, came to London at this time in order to take leave officially. Herbert Bismarck was well qualified by his exceptional position, both in Germany and in England, to deal with the matter of Angra Pequena. Not only was his personal position unique, but he was well acquainted with London, had served there for some time in a diplomatic post, and had made a position for himself in London society which enabled him not only to pick up confidential information for his father but to discuss in London frankly and unofficially, and with the most important people, the problems at issue between the two governments.† He was also more vigorous than Münster in standing up for the German side of the argument. It had been Bismarck's complaint that Münster was unwilling to make an unfriendly or discourteous communication, and had therefore refrained from making the German position entirely clear to the British Government. Herbert, in his anxiety to remedy matters, appears to have committed excesses in the opposite direction. There are many instances of the overbearing qualities

* 10 June 1884. Prince Bismarck to Count Münster. German White Book, *Angra Pequena,* No. 24.

† See Appendix III.

and lack of tact which he showed on other occasions,* and several sources indicate that on this mission also he exceeded the bounds of diplomatic convention and acted with deliberate rudeness. This was perhaps a desired effect, since the chief reason for sending Herbert Bismarck to London at this time was probably that Münster had not represented German interests with sufficient energy.

In his first conversation with Lord Granville, on 14 June 1884, Count Herbert Bismarck complained of the long delay in answering the chancellor's inquiries, "to which replies might to all appearance have been given in three days." He refused to recognize any authority but the foreign office with which the German Government could negotiate, and, besides this, accused Lord Derby of double-dealing. "In this case," Lord Granville quoted him as saying, "not only was the delay in answering objectionable in itself, but it appeared that Lord Derby had availed himself of it to press the Government of the Cape Colony to take steps with a view to anticipate any action on the part of the German Government." Such a charge Lord Granville emphatically denied. "It was a complete misunderstanding of Lord Derby's action," he replied, "to suppose that his action in consulting the Government of the Cape Colony was intended in any sense to be hostile to the German Government. On the contrary, he had acted in the belief derived from some of the questions which had been asked by the German Government that it was their desire that the German settlers should receive British protection." Count Herbert Bismarck recapitulated the history of the communications which had passed between the two governments, and explained that his father could not refuse protection to German subjects whose interests had been established in a district which had been described in despatches presented to Parliament as being outside the limits of the British colony. He admitted, as has been stated in an earlier chapter, that the views of the German Government had not been expressed so clearly as might have been done, and said that they did not

* See Appendix III.

intend to establish "State Colonies," but wished to give "full protection to Germans settling in uncivilized countries which were not under the Sovereign jurisdiction of other European States" (3). Prince Bismarck later objected to the passage where the remark about "State Colonies" was ascribed to his son, and at his request this passage was stricken out of the report of this conversation that appeared in the British Blue Book.* Count Herbert Bismarck relates that in this interview Granville also inquired whether Germany would proclaim her sovereignty. Count Bismarck replied evasively that they would probably act as England had done in Borneo, and wrote home to ask his father whether he might enter into this question (4). But this was a question of less importance, and Herbert Bismarck had undoubtedly achieved a fair success in his first interview. He had made clear to the British Government the importance that Bismarck attached to Angra Pequena, and he had also made clear, what Granville had apparently not realized until now, that his father intended to set up such an arrangement at Angra Pequena as would exclude the possibility of the annexation of that place by another power, in other words an arrangement which would be, irrespective of the question of sovereignty, equivalent to annexation. Acquired rights of the subjects of other nations, he said, when Granville brought this question up, would as a matter of course be scrupulously respected.

One other subject was discussed in this conversation of 14 June 1884. Count Herbert Bismarck observed, in regard to the Egyptian question, that his father thought Lord Granville should be warned "that the feeling in Germany as regards these colonial questions was so strong that with the best wishes he felt he should be unable to afford us the same friendly assistance as hitherto, unless he could give some satisfaction to public opinion on the subject." Granville replied that he "objected to anything in the nature of a bargain between us. Each question ought to be discussed on its own merits" (5). The tone of his reply suggests that the idea was

* See Appendix II.

a new one to him, a fact that throws an unfavorable light upon Münster's execution of his instructions, in which this idea had been put forward again and again. Count Herbert Bismarck insisted that there was no question of a bargain, "we simply claim a right." To this Lord Granville replied: "If it is your *right* you will see England at your feet at once." He promised to press the matter forward as fast as possible, and expressed his strong desire to come to a satisfactory settlement (4). The question, he said, affected his colleagues more than it did him, and he invited Count Bismarck to confer, in his presence, with Lord Derby and Lord Kimberley, an invitation which was curtly refused. He denied having had any report from Ampthill on a conversation with Prince Bismarck on 9 June 1884, and was greatly surprised when Herbert Bismarck informed him that German interests in Egypt amounted to more than a hundred million marks.*

But Herbert Bismarck's representations, though they opened Lord Granville's mind, were not immediately effectual. Dilke relates that on 14 June 1884 he attended a cabinet meeting at Lord Granville's house. Herbert Bismarck was also in the house, and "had been very rude to Lord Granville about Angra Pequena, which was mentioned to the Cabinet, which would do nothing."†

On 17 June 1884, when Count Herbert Bismarck saw Lord Granville for the second time, he again brought up the subject of his father's conversation with Lord Ampthill on 9 June. On this occasion, Granville called in his private secretary, and a long search was made through a number of despatch boxes, but no trace was found of any message from Ampthill of the kind described, except a private letter of 10 June, which at present lay before Lord Derby.‡ But this letter, when it was found, proved to be mostly about Egypt. Two months before, Bismarck had told Lord Ampthill that "Germany's financial interests in the Caisse did not exceed

* 16 June 1884. Count Herbert Bismarck to Prince Bismarck. *Die Grosse Politik,* IV, No. 745.

† Gwynn and Tuckwell: *Life of Sir Charles W. Dilke,* II, 81.

‡ 17 June 1884. Count Herbert Bismarck to Prince Bismarck. *Die Grosse Politik,* IV, No. 746.

a miserable million of marks."* When he received the British ambassador on 9 June, he told a very different story. "The financial arrangements, he said,—created greater interest in Southern Germany than he had anticipated, and he had been surprized to receive petitions from Francfort Financers [sic] assuring him that more than one hundred millions of Marks of German money were invested in Egyptian securities." In regard to Angra Pequena, Ampthill merely added that he was glad Granville proposed to have a full discussion with Herbert Bismarck on the question, "which is a burning one, and calculated to give us much trouble with Germany."† Ampthill did not mention that Bismarck had brought up Angra Pequena in the conversation at all.

But on 14 June Lord Ampthill saw Bismarck again, and had a long talk with him about the Angra Pequena question. Bismarck explained that a debate was that day beginning in the Reichstag in which he might be asked about this matter. He feared that a bad impression would be made on German public opinion if the British Government could not suggest a satisfactory solution. He discussed the negotiations in a very earnest spirit, and deplored the delay in answering his questions, "which he said had been respectfully and loyally put to Her Majesty's Government." He anticipated that the national feeling of Germany would become less cordial than heretofore, and would seek to influence his foreign policy. Finally he requested Lord Ampthill to telegraph to Granville and beg him "for the sake of international good will to give Count Münster an answer which he could communicate to the German Reichstag without adding fuel to the fire" (6).

Ampthill telegraphed to Granville, as requested, on the same day, 14 June 1884 (7).

In order to understand the attitude of the British Government at this time, it must be remembered that up till now they had been entirely convinced that Bismarck had not the

* 10 April 1884. Lord Ampthill to Lord Granville. Lord Edmond Fitzmaurice: *Life of Lord Granville,* II, 339.

† 10 June 1884. Lord Ampthill to Lord Granville. Private. Private Granville MSS, G.D. 29/178.

slightest interest in colonial ventures. The process of disillusionment was necessarily laborious and slow. The news received from Ampthill had no doubt made an alteration in Lord Granville's views, but in the interview with Count Herbert Bismarck that followed, on 17 June 1884, Granville was still inclined to gossip over the matter, to ask again and again for details as to the exact nature of Germany's plans, and to repeat that he had always believed that Germany really wanted England to give protection to Angra Pequena.

Herbert Bismarck was primed for this interview by a telegram from his father, of 16 June 1884, replying to his inquiry as to whether he might discuss the question of sovereignty with Lord Granville. Prince Bismarck said that whether he proclaimed sovereignty or not depended upon circumstances, even upon accidents. But in any case this was no business of England's, if she had no sovereignty at Angra Pequena herself, which was the only question he had asked of her. He personally was thinking of granting a charter, but refused to make a statement binding him for the future (8).

Thus, when Lord Granville brought up the subject of sovereignty on 17 June, Herbert Bismarck retorted that he thought it "a question of mere curiosity if you ask about the sovereignty: it can be all the same to you, what another power does in a country not belonging to you." He added that he was sure "that my Government would decline to give an answer in a matter that is of no concern for you." On this passage Prince Bismarck commented, in the margin of his son's despatch, "right."

Granville went on to say that in England it was the opinion that the national possessions were already too great. He added that Derby's explanation to the deputation of South African merchants was founded on the belief that Germany wished England to annex Angra Pequena. But England had not the slightest reason to oppose German colonization, and would only trouble about the acquired rights of English firms. He promised that the new Cape Government, which was much more chauvinistic than the old one, would be instructed by telegram to take no further step for the time being.*

Such was Count Herbert Bismarck's account of the conversation. Lord Granville's was rather different, and, according to it, the foreign secretary's questions about German sovereignty had considerable point. He wrote to Ampthill that he had asked Herbert Bismarck to let him know definitely what Germany claimed. "Did they wish, I said, to protect the German settlers only, or were they desirious of undertaking the protection of both the German and the British settlers, or thirdly—did they claim to extend protection to all settlers of whatever nationality who might obtain concessions.

"Count H. Bismarck promised to let me have an answer on the subject."† Later, on 17 June, Lord Granville wrote the German embassy to ask what was the extent of the territory which Germany wished to take under her protection, whether it included only the acquisitions of Lüderitz, or also the possessions of the English firm, or still more. Münster immediately telegraphed these questions to Berlin (9). In a telegraphic reply of 18 June, Bismarck declared that Germany would of course respect acquired rights, and also had no intention of founding a penal settlement, but he refused to make any statement as to his intentions, because he feared that the frankness with which he had acted formerly would be abused, now that England had left unanswered for six months the German inquiries respecting her possessions, in order to use the intervening time in the attempt to increase them (10).

But before Herbert Bismarck saw Lord Granville again, the British Government had come to a decision. In his notes on the meetings of the cabinet, Sir Charles Dilke wrote that on 21 June 1884 "Angra Pequena was mentioned, and it was decided that Bismarck, who was greatly irritated with the Government, was to have all he wanted."‡

* 17 June 1884. Count Herbert Bismarck to Prince Bismarck. *Die Grosse Politik,* IV, No. 746. See also Appendix III.

† 18 June 1884. Lord Granville to Lord Ampthill. No. 178. Confidential. Draft. F.O. 64/1102.

‡ Gwynn and Tuckwell: *Life of Sir Charles W. Dilke,* II, 81.

Granville confidentially informed Count Herbert Bismarck of this decision the next day, 22 June. He said that he had read to the cabinet Count Münster's note of 31 December 1883, as well as the former official declarations in respect to the extent of British sovereignty in South Africa. The cabinet agreed with Granville that misunderstandings on both sides had occurred, "but after careful consideration of all the communications which had passed and of the circumstances of the case they had come to the conclusion that we were not in a position to question the right of the German Government to afford protection to its own subjects who had settled there." They desired, however, that the rights of British subjects should be respected. There might be certain disputed claims, as Lord Granville did not know how far the intended German protection would extend. Count Herbert Bismarck replied that acquired rights would of course be respected, but he added, in accordance with Prince Bismarck's telegram of 18 June, that the German Government were not yet in a position to answer Lord Granville's questions as to the extent to which they wished to exercise sovereignty, and could on no account make a binding statement in regard to this. He said further, according to his own account of the conversation, that the fact that the well-grounded English claims would be respected was all that the British Government needed to know (11). The decision of the British Government was immediately telegraphed by Münster to Berlin.*

Having thus achieved in three interviews a preliminary settlement of the Angra Pequena question, Count Herbert Bismarck postponed the details for a short while, and turned his attention to the other members of the British cabinet. Several of these had hardly been informed at all of the negotiations until Herbert Bismarck took them over on 14 June, and were much surprised at the more detailed accounts which he now gave them, and annoyed at the policy which had been followed by Lord Granville and Lord Derby. In

* 22 June 1884. Count Münster to German foreign office. Telegram. German White Book, *Angra Pequena,* No. 27.

his despatch of 22 June, Herbert Bismarck reported that he had recently had a meal at the house of Sir William Harcourt, who asked him if it were true that England's Egyptian policy had antagonized Germany. Herbert Bismarck replied that his father had very different grounds for his annoyance, and briefly recounted to the home secretary the negotiations over Fiji and Angra Pequena. At this Harcourt exclaimed (as Herbert Bismarck reported him): "Good God, I had no idea of this, you may have the whole of Fidji if you like, I think it ridiculous if we offer the slightest difficulties to you in these questions." In a later conversation, on 22 June, he confided to Count Herbert Bismarck that the cabinet's decision of the day before had been taken unanimously and without discussion. Up to now, he said, most of the ministers had known nothing about the question at all, and he himself didn't yet know where Angra Pequena was. But they had immediately understood the position of the German Government, and only wished to wipe out the bad impression left by the stupidity of the colonial office. The only question that remained to be settled was the one of sovereignty, and he thought it would be best if Germany annexed the place outright. He begged that Germany would help the British Government in their difficulties with Parliament: "There have been some declarations lately, that might create us difficulties in Parliament, and I trust you will help us to get out of them without humiliation."

This hope was also expressed by Granville, in his conversation with Herbert Bismarck on 22 June which has already been described. Herbert Bismarck quotes him as saying: "We have decided to take this line, but we are in a sort of mess: it is all the fault of the Colonial Office and of Lord Derby, who have talked about the matter without consulting me and giving it due consideration."* Lord Derby had indeed freely and irresponsibly discussed the question in his public statements, both in the House of Lords and elsewhere, and had

* 22 June 1884. Count Herbert Bismarck to Prince Bismarck. *Die Grosse Politik,* IV, No. 747.

always taken the line that Bismarck on no account wished to acquire Angra Pequena for Germany, and that England could exclude any foreign power from the coast. The cabinet now realized that these statements were going to be difficult to explain away.

The embarrassment of the British Government was due in the first place to the policy of Lord Granville. Instead of taking the lead, as a foreign secretary was bound to do in such an important question of foreign policy, he had completely delegated his authority to another member of the cabinet. But if Granville allowed too much influence on foreign policy to one member of the cabinet, he sinned equally far in the opposite direction, for, until June 1884, he does not appear to have consulted the other members of the cabinet at all. Harcourt's statement that the Angra Pequena question was entirely new to most of the ministers is incredible on the face of it, but, as far as it is possible to trace the matter in the documents, this statement was well founded. Kimberley and Northbrook may have known something about what was happening, as they both replied for the government to questions regarding Angra Pequena on 13 June and 19 June respectively. But this was late in the day. There is nothing in the Private Granville Papers or in the Gladstone Papers to show that any member of the cabinet was consulted as to the attitude which should be maintained towards Germany in this matter before June 1884. The first mention of Angra Pequena to be found in Gladstone's private correspondence is in a letter from Gladstone to Granville of 5 September 1884. There is nothing to show that Gladstone was consulted at all before June 1884, when the question came up in the cabinet, which is most extraordinary in view of the interest Gladstone took in foreign affairs and the influence he exerted upon them. In later colonial controversies with Germany, when the cabinet was more fully informed, Gladstone took an important, indeed almost decisive, part in the negotiations, and his later correspondence is full of references to New Guinea, which makes his silence in regard to Angra Pequena all the more striking.*

The explanation of Granville's policy is of course his failure to recognize the significance of the German communications, a matter which has already been fully discussed. Deluded by his fixed belief that Bismarck was unalterably opposed to colonies, he failed to answer the German inquiries as to England's title to Angra Pequena, and shifted the responsibility to the colonial office. Derby, whose mistakes were as notable as Lord Granville's, concluded that the German Government desired a British annexation, and hence that the matter was one which should be left entirely to the discretion of the Cape Colony, which he was anxious to oblige in any case. As is natural when two people are directing negotiations which should be authoritatively handled, both men took the matter too easily. Granville avoided responsibility, and Derby abused the responsibility that had been handed over to him. When the other members of the cabinet were drawn into the negotiations, partly through the agency of Herbert Bismarck, British policy, though it did not even then become either unanimous or consistent, underwent a marked change.

The preliminary agreement that had been reached between Count Herbert Bismarck and Lord Granville caused a certain amount of satisfaction in Berlin. Lord Ampthill wrote that Prince Bismarck had expressed to him his gratitude for being given an answer "just in time to bowl over his enemies, Bamberger and Richter, in the Budget Commission," and went on to say: "The press is all praise at the fairness, justice, and friendliness of your decision, and I hear from all sides that it has done immense good to our international relations; for the Germans had set their hearts on the protection of Herr Lüderitz's enterprise at Angra Pequena."† Bismarck's satis-

* See Appendix IV.

† 28 June 1884. Lord Ampthill to Lord Granville. Lord Edmond Fitzmaurice: *Life of Lord Granville,* II, 355.

faction, however, which was perhaps optimistically exaggerated by Lord Ampthill, was of short duration.

Count Herbert Bismarck had succeeded in persuading the British Government to accept the situation created by Germany at Angra Pequena, and when, on 30 June 1884, Viscount Sidmouth brought the matter up in the House of Lords yet another time, Granville replied that Her Majesty's Government, after considering all the circumstances of the case and more especially "the declarations made some years ago by the Government as to the limits of the Cape Colony, came to the conclusion that it was not possible nor desirable for them to oppose the protection of the German Empire being extended to German subjects having establishments in Angra Pequena."* But while Herbert Bismarck had dealt with the British Government competently on the main issues, his handling of the details does not appear to have been so satisfactory. The British Government did not yet fully appreciate the situation, and in this same speech Granville added that a formal recognition of the German protection would follow as soon as an agreement could be made which would secure acquired rights and would prevent any chance of a convict establishment being founded there. The last suggestion was to cause more friction in the near future.

England had now agreed to the German position, and a settlement might have been reached along the lines of Lord Granville's conversations with Herbert Bismarck, had not the British Government with almost incredible blindness taken two steps which antagonized Bismarck more than ever. In the first place Granville used language at Berlin that gave the impression that England would agree to the German claims only on the condition that Bismarck give a pledge that he would not found a penal settlement at Angra Pequena. Far more important than this, Lord Derby, with the assent of the British foreign office, encouraged the Cape Colony to annex certain parts of South West Africa adjacent to Angra

* 30 June 1884. *Hansard Parliamentary Debates,* 3rd Series, CCLXXXIX, 1655.

Pequena which had not been explicitly claimed by Bismarck. This was as ill-advised an action as the British Government could have taken, and to show how it came about we must go back a little and explain what was happening in the Cape Colony and the colonial office.

Feeling in the Cape Colony was now running high. The change of attitude of the government in London did not extend to the ministers in Cape Town, and in the middle of July 1884 Bismarck's annoyance was increased by the arrival of a report from the German consul in Cape Town announcing that the Cape premier had recently informed him that he was aware the German Government had no intention of making an annexation, desired only that order should exist at Angra Pequena, and would be pleased if the Cape Colony took the place. The premier proposed to introduce a bill shortly to the Cape Parliament, which should bring about this annexation.* Hatzfeldt, in sending this despatch on to Münster, remarked that it confirmed the German suspicions that the instructions sent from London to Cape Town had given the impression that Germany desired an extension of British sovereignty.†

Up to this time, however, the British Government had acted loyally. True to the promise made by Lord Granville to Count Herbert Bismarck on 17 June 1884, Derby had telegraphed on the same day to the governor of the Cape Colony not to bring forward the vote for the control of Angra Pequena at present, "in order to avoid any misunderstanding between Her Majesty's Government and German Ministry, with whom communications are proceeding."‡ But much pressure was brought to bear upon Lord Derby from the Cape Colony as well as from Mr. De Pass in England, in the month that followed. On 26 June a despatch arrived from Sir Hercules

* 4 June 1884. Lippert, the German consul in Cape Town, to Prince Bismarck. German White Book, *Angra Pequena,* No. 28.

† 11 July 1884. Count Hatzfeldt to Count Münster. German White Book, *Angra Pequena,* No. 29.

‡ 17 June 1884. Lord Derby to Sir Hercules Robinson. Telegram. British Blue Book, (C. 4190), No. 60.

Robinson, enclosing a long minute from the ministers of the Cape Colony dated 29 May, and giving their opinion that some extension of British jurisdiction on the southwest coast of Africa was unavoidable. The ministers declared that only two courses were open, the protection or the annexation of the coast line in question. They themselves would prefer protection, but were quite ready for either alternative.*

On 26 June 1884 Mr. De Pass sent to the colonial office a violent and indignant letter, protesting bitterly against the claim of Herr Lüderitz to dispossess him after he had spent over 300,000 pounds in developing the country.† His letter was forwarded to the foreign office on 27 June, with the comment that Lord Derby thought an inquiry in the conflicting claims should be made by an English and a German commissioner jointly.‡ Pauncefote agreed to this, and thought that the sooner the matter was settled by a commission on the spot the better (12).

De Pass reinforced his plea on 4 July 1884 by announcing that he had other establishments along the same coast, at Hottentot Bay and Sandwich Harbor. He begged that telegraphic instructions might be sent for the annexation of the entire coast line.§

Lord Derby now decided to adopt a plan which he apparently hoped would satisfy both the German Government and the colonists. In a letter from the colonial office to the foreign office of 8 July 1884 it was stated that Lord Derby proposed, "with Earl Granville's concurrence," to telegraph to the Cape that the British Government were not in a position to oppose Germany's intention to confer protection upon the acquisitions of Lüderitz. "Lord Derby proposes to add, however, that Her Majesty's Government will be prepared to proclaim British protection and authority over any other

* 29 May 1884. Minute by the ministers of the Cape Colony. British Blue Book, (C. 4190), No. 63, Enclosure.

† 26 June 1884. Daniel De Pass to colonial office. *Ibid.*, No. 64.

‡ 27 June 1884. Colonial office to foreign office. *Ibid.*, No. 65.

§ 4 July 1884. Daniel De Pass to colonial office. British Blue Book, (C. 4190), No. 68.

places on the coast at which British subjects have concessions or establishments if the Cape Parliament will make the necessary provision for the cost." Since De Pass, in his last letter, claimed to have establishments at Sandwich Harbor and Hottentot Bay, Lord Derby proposed "to point this out to Sir Hercules Robinson, adding that it is inferred that the Cape Government will desire British protection over the coast north of M. Lüderitz's concession, which is said to extend to latitude 26."* In other words, Lord Derby proposed to invite the Cape Colony to seize without delay all the territory on this coast which had not yet been specifically placed under German protection. Such an act was, of course, legally justifiable, since this territory was still technically vacant, but it was, at the very least, ungracious to attempt to restrict the first beginnings of German colonization by immediately annexing the territory adjacent to that which Germany had just acquired.

But the foreign office saw nothing objectionable in this step. On 11 July Sir Julian Pauncefote wrote in a minute that it would be quite in accordance with the line which the foreign office proposed to take (13). Pressure on Lord Derby was increased when, on 9 July, a telegram arrived from the Cape Colony saying that Parliament would soon be prorogued, and that the ministers were anxiously awaiting the decision of the British Government. The feeling in the colony, it was stated, was strongly in favor of the establishment of British authority over the coast line from the Orange River upwards, and the annexation of Damaraland to the German Empire was greatly deprecated.† This information, which was forwarded to the foreign office on 10 July,‡ apparently made such a strong impression upon Lord Derby that on 14 July he sent off the proposed telegram to the Cape without waiting for the concurrence of Lord Granville for which he

* 8 July 1884. Colonial office to foreign office. British Blue Book, (C. 4190), No. 70.

† 9 July 1884. Sir Hercules Robinson to Lord Derby. Telegram. *Ibid.*, No. 71.

‡ 10 July 1884. Colonial office to foreign office. *Ibid.*, No. 72.

had asked, and which did not actually arrive until the following day.* In his telegram to the Cape of 14 July Derby explained that England could not oppose the German intentions in regard to Angra Pequena, but added: "Her Majesty's Government will be prepared proclaim under British protection and authority any other places on the coast at which British subjects have claims, if Colonial legislature will make arrangements for cost.

"De Pass stated that he has claims at Sandwich Bay and Hottentot Bay as well as Angra Pequena. Her Majesty's Government infer Colonial Government will consider it desirable that coast up to the north of Lüderitz concession . . . should be placed under British protection."†

The effect of these promptings on the Cape Government, and the consequent action of Bismarck must be considered in the next chapter. There were other negotiations going on at the same time which demand immediate attention.

On 14 July 1884 Lord Granville sent a despatch to Ampthill which formed the basis of a note handed in by Ampthill to the German foreign office on 19 July. This despatch stated that the British Government had come to the conclusion that the German claim to protect German subjects at Angra Pequena could not be contested, and they were therefore prepared to recognize Germany's right to give this protection "as soon as proper arrangements can be agreed upon between the two Governments for giving security against the formation of any penal settlement upon any part of the coast in question, and for making provision for the recognition of acquired rights, and the protection of the interests of British subjects who may hold concessions, or carry on trade in those parts." It was added that the best way of settling all conflicting claims would probably be to nominate an Anglo-German commission.‡

* 15 July 1884. Foreign office to colonial office. British Blue Book, (C. 4190), No. 76.

† 14 July 1884. Lord Derby to Sir Hercules Robinson. Telegram. *Ibid.*, No. 74.

‡ 14 July 1884. Lord Granville to Lord Ampthill. British Blue Book, (C. 4190), No. 75, Enclosure.

The wording of this despatch was imprudent. It gave the impression that England, while recognizing the German claims and the justice of the German position, was trying to obtain as a condition of this recognition a pledge from Bismarck not to establish a penal settlement. It was wholly outside of sound diplomatic tradition for the British Government, at the end of a series of negotiations in which they had been defeated, to attempt to impose a condition which they were not prepared to enforce. Above all was this unwise when Bismarck was obviously in an unfriendly and irritable state of mind. Granville later denied that he had sought to impose a condition. He said that he merely wished to know for certain, what he had already been told unofficially, that Germany had no intention of placing a convict establishment so near to an important British colony. If this was what he meant it was tactlessly expressed and Bismarck keenly resented it. Granville's object was probably to secure a statement which would partially save England's face with the colonists. It would appear that he was misled in this matter by his conversations with Count Herbert Bismarck. (See page 117.) The latter, fresh from London, appreciated the British attitude. He had received a copy of Granville's despatch just before he left London,* and on 14 July he wrote to his father from The Hague to explain that in his opinion the words "security against the formation etc." were merely a *façon de parler,* introduced into the despatch because it would be published in a Blue Book. He himself, in accordance with his instructions, had told Lord Granville that the German Government had no intention of founding a penal settlement at Angra Pequena, and he thought a reference to this conversation would be a sufficient reply to Lord Granville's request, since the British Government had no intention of exacting an obligation from Germany. "The English government," he wrote, "is meeting severe difficulties with Australia because of the French penal settlement in New Caledonia, and it is only in consideration

* 13 July 1884. Lord Granville to Count Herbert Bismarck. Draft. Private. Private Granville MSS, G.D. 29/207.

of that that they bring forward this question in regard to Angra Pequena" (14).

Herbert Bismarck had found time to leave a copy of Lord Granville's despatch at the German embassy in London before he left, and on 14 July Count Münster sent it to Berlin.* Bismarck, who was in Varzin at the time, telegraphed to the foreign office in Berlin on 16 July that if Lord Ampthill should hand in the promised note about Angra Pequena he should immediately be told confidentially that Germany could not accept conditions in the exercise of her own rights. The protection of English subjects was a matter of course, and he had no intention of establishing a penal settlement, but to allow this to be imposed as a condition was inconsistent with the dignity of Germany as a sovereign power (15).

On 19 July 1884 Lord Ampthill addressed to the German foreign office a note which was the answer to Count Münster's note to the British foreign office of 31 December 1883. Ampthill's note gave the information that was in Granville's despatch of 14 July, that the British Government were prepared to recognize Germany's right to protect Angra Pequena as soon as arrangements could be made for giving security against a penal settlement.† In reply, Count Hatzfeldt told Lord Ampthill that while the German Government adhered to their expressed intention not to establish a penal settlement, "that assurance could not be made a condition of the proposed arrangment between the two Governments in his opinion."‡ The matter was taken up more fully in a vigorous despatch from Bismarck a few days later.

* 14 July 1884. Count Münster to Prince Bismarck. Reichsarchiv, Vermischtes Südwestafrika IV.

† 19 July 1884. Lord Ampthill to Count Hatzfeldt. British Blue Book, (C. 4262), second part of Enclosure 1 in No. 2.

‡ 25 July 1884. Lord Ampthill to Lord Granville. *Ibid.*, first part of Enclosure 1 in No. 2.

NOTES

1. June 1884. Draft note to Count Münster. Marked: "Suspended." F.O. 64/1102.

"I regret the delay which has occurred in replying to your Excellency's communication of the 31st of December last upon the subject of the Sovereignty of Angra Pequena, but the delay has been unavoidable owing to the necessity of communicating with the Government of the Cape.

"I have now the honour to acquaint your Excellency that after careful consideration, and communication with the Government of the Cape Colony, Her Majesty's Government have decided that arrangements shall be made for giving protection under the British flag to any persons, German as well as English, who may have duly acquired concessions, or established commercial enterprises, on that portion of the coast of Africa, which lies between the Orange River and Walwich [sic] Bay."

(The note goes on to suggest the settlement of disputed claims by a joint commission.)

2. 15 June 1884. Minute by Sir Julian Pauncefote. F.O. 64/1102.

"Angra Pequena.

"Lord Granville has decided to suspend action in this matter until he has spoken to Count Herbert Bismarck who is daily expected in London."

3. 14 June 1884. Lord Granville to Lord Ampthill. British Blue Book, (C. 4190), No. 69, Enclosure. Full version in F.O. 64/1102, despatch No. 169A. Draft. The words omitted from the Blue Book are given below, in their context, and are indicated by italics.

"It was evident that there had been some misunderstanding on both sides. *Count Bismarck admitted that the views of the German Government had not perhaps been quite so clearly stated as might have been done.* In answer to questions put by me, he stated that *it was not the intention of the German Government to establish State Colonies anywhere, but that* they wished to give full protection to Germans settling in uncivilized countries which were not under the Sovereign jurisdiction of other European States."

4. 14 June 1884. Count Herbert Bismarck to Prince Bismarck. Reichsarchiv, Vermischtes Südwestafrika III.

" . . . Ich verwerthete Alles, was in den letzten Erlassen hierher gesagt ist, was ich angewiesen worden bin auszusprechen und betonte die Richtung unserer Politik, die bisherige wie die etwaige zukünftige. Granville sagte 'you are quite right in telling that to me, but I will not repeat it to my colleagues, because the thing would look as a bargain.' 'Not in the least,' sagte ich 'there is no bargain in question, we simply claim a right. There is a res nullius, as appears from your note of november 21st 1883 and from instructions sent out from here to your people in the years 1880 and 1881. We have the painful impression, that you will evade the question and are awaiting reports, whether you can want the thing.' Dies bestritt Granville heftig und sagte 'if it is your *right* you will see England at your feet at once.'

" . . . Dann fragte er noch 'will you proclaim your sovereignty?' Ich erwiederte ausweichend, wir würden wohl ähnlich handeln, wie sie in Borneo. 'well,' said he 'there we have *not* proclaimed sovereignty, only given a charter.'

" . . . Soll ich auf die Frage wegen 'sovereignty' am nächsten Dienstag noch eingehen?"

5. 14 June 1884. Lord Granville to Lord Ampthill. No. 169B. Confidential. Draft. F.O. 64/1102.

"In the course of the conversation reported in my previous Despatch of this day's date Count Herbert Bismarck observed that while Prince Bismarck still entertained the same friendly feelings towards Her Majesty's Government, and was desirous of supporting their policy in Egypt, His Highness thought it right that I should be warned that the feeling in Germany as regards these colonial questions was so strong that with the best wishes he felt he should be unable to afford us the same friendly assistance as hitherto, unless he could give some satisfaction to public opinion on the subject.

"I said that I objected to anything in the nature of a bargain between us. Each question ought to be discussed on its own merits.

" . . . Count H. Bismarck said that he did not raise any question of bargain, but the German Government expected their rights to be respected.

"I replied that if the German Government had rights, which we, on examination could admit, Count H. Bismarck might be sure that we should not only do so, but be ready to meet the German Government with great cordiality in the matter."

6. 14 June 1884. Lord Ampthill to Lord Granville. Private. Private Granville MSS, G.D. 29/178.

"I have just seen Prince Bismarck who begged of me to tell you that the Debate begins to day in Parliament in which he may be asked about the Angra Pequena question. He fears that deep and lasting disappointment will be felt by Public Opinion in Germany if H.M.G. cannot suggest a satisfactory settlement of the question. He talked over the various phases of the negotiations in London between Count Münster and Her Majesty's Government in a very earnest but always courteous spirit,—deplored the delay in answering his questions, which he said had been respectfully and loyally put to Her Majesty's Government, and feared that Public Opinion in Germany would deeply resent the fact that after six months delay the Cape Government had been 'wedged in' between German aspirations and interests and Angra Pequena.

"His own feelings of friendship towards England could never change,—but the national feeling of Germany would, he anticipated, become less cordial than heretofore and would seek to influence his foreign policy. He ended by requesting me to telegraph to you and beg of you for the sake of international good will to give Count Münster an answer which he could communicate to the German Reichstag without adding fuel to the fire. . . ."

7. 14 June 1884. Lord Ampthill to Lord Granville. Cipher telegram. Private. Private Granville MSS, G.D. 29/178.

"Prince Bismarck desires me to tell you the debate begins to-day in Parliament in which he may be asked about Angra Pequena question.

"He fears that deep and lasting disappointment will be felt by public opinion in Germany if H.M. Govt. cannot suggest a satisfactory settlement of the question."

8. 16 June 1884. Prince Bismarck to Count Herbert Bismarck. Cipher telegram. No. 39. Reichsarchiv, Vermischtes Südwestafrika III.

"Brief vom 14. erhalten.

"Ob wir Souveränetät proklamiren hängt von Umständen, sogar von Zufällen ab. Ich weiss aber nicht, was England das angeht, wenn es selbst keine Souveränetät dort hat; die Frage für uns war nur, ob England seine Souveränetät dort bereits irgendwie proclamirt hatte. Diese Frage hat England wiederholt verneint. Ich habe auch nicht gefragt, ob England in Zukunft schützen wolle, sondern ob es bislang dort über die Macht zu schützen verfüge. 1880 fragten wir wegen Schutz rheinischer Missionen allerdings an; die ablehnende Antwort Granvilles ist vom 29 November 1880. Für meine Person denke ich bis jetzt nur an Charter, lehne aber ab Verpflichtungen einzugehen."

9. 17 June 1884. Count Münster to German foreign office. Cipher telegram. No. 74. Reichsarchiv, Vermischtes Südwestafrika III.

" . . . Lord Granville schreibt eben, 'welches ist die Ausdehnung des

Gebiets, das Deutschland unter Protection nehmen will; (Bismarck, in margin: das weiss nur Lüderitz; wir werden schützen, was er rite erwirbt.) erstreckt es sich nur auf die Erwerbungen von Lüderitz oder auch auf den Besitz der Englischen Firma oder umfasst es noch mehr?' (Bismarck: Controlle nicht annehmbar.)"

10. 18 June 1884. Prince Bismarck to Count Münster. Cipher telegram. No. 43. Reichsarchiv, Vermischtes Südwestafrika III.

"Telegramm No. 74 erhalten. Dass wir die droits acquis englischer Unterthanen respektiren, ist selbstverständlich; wir werden das englische Verfahren in Fidji nicht nachahmen. Auch liegen Verbrechercolonien nicht in unserer Absicht. . . . Auf Lord Granville's Frage nach der beabsichtigten Ausdehnung unserer Protection würde ich bei entgegenkommenderer und offenerer Behandlung der Sache von englischer Seite *früher* gern geantwortet haben, jetzt lehne ich diese Controlle unserer Absichten ab, da ich Missbrauch der Offenheit, mit welcher ich früher die Sache behandelt habe, fürchte, nachdem unsere Anfrage über Englands Besitzstand sechs Monate lang unbeantwortet geblieben ist, um inzwischen die Vergrösserung desselben zu versuchen. Vorstehender Wortlaut ist natürlich nicht zur Mittheilung, sondern zu Ew. pp. Orientirung bestimmt."

11. Count Herbert Bismarck's account of this conversation is contained in his despatch to Prince Bismarck dated 22 June 1884, *Die Grosse Politik,* IV, No. 747. Granville's account is his despatch to Lord Ampthill No. 180, Confidential, of the same date, F.O. 64/1102. The most important passage of this has been quoted in the text, but the following one is also of interest.

"He referred to the question I had put to him respecting the extent to which the German Government claimed to exercise protection in Angra Pequena, and said that they had a difficulty in answering until they were more perfectly informed of all the local circumstances, but that in any case it was their intention and desire to respect acquired rights."

12. 28 June 1884. Minute by Sir Julian Pauncefote. F.O. 64/1102.

"Mr. de Pass makes out a strong case against the claim of the Germans to dispossess him & the sooner the matter is settled by a commission on the spot, the better.

"The C.O. proposals as to the next step are now before Lord Granville."

13. 11 July 1884. Minute by Sir Julian Pauncefote. F.O. 64/1102.

"Lord Granville,

"It seems to me that there can be no objection to the C.O. sending the Tel. proposed in their letter of 8 July. It is quite in accordance with the Draft proposals we are addressing to them on the subject and which you will find in this Box."

14. 14 July 1884. Count Herbert Bismarck, at The Hague, to Prince Bismarck. Reichsarchiv, Vermischtes Südwestafrika IV.

"Euerer Durchlaucht beehre ich mich beifolgendes Schreiben Lord Granville's nebst Anlage, welches mir kurz vor meiner gestrigen Abreise von London zuging, ganz gehorsamst einzureichen. Abschrift der an Lord Ampthill gerichteten Note habe ich noch auf der Londoner Botschaft zurücklassen können, mich aber enthalten meinerseits Lord Granville eine Empfangsbestätigung zugehen zu lassen.

"Was die Worte auf der zweiten Seite unten 'security against the formation etc.' betrifft, so sehe ich dieselben nur als eine façon de parler an, welche in den Erlass an Lord Ampthill mit Rücksicht auf das Blaubuch aufgenommen sind. Wie aus dem von London eingereichten ersten Erlass an Lord Ampthill vom 14ten v.M. ersichtlich ist, hatte ich auf Lord Granville's

Befragen nach Massgabe von Euerer Durchlaucht Instructionen nur gesagt 'dass wir nicht die Absicht hätten, eine Verbrechercolonie in Angra Pequena zu errichten.' Meines gehorsamsten Dafürhaltens dürfte ein Verweis auf jene mündliche Mittheilung genügen, da der englischen Regierung ja in keiner Weise ein Anspruch zusteht, irgend eine Servitut auf unter Deutscher Protection stehendes Gebiet einzutragen wenn diese Servitut auch noch so sehr Formsprache und imperativ ist.

"Die englische Regierung geht unangenehmen Schwierigkeiten mit Australien wegen der französischen Verbrecher-Kolonie in Neu-Caledonien entgegen und mit Rücksicht darauf regt sie nur diese Frage für Angra Pequena an. Ich darf mir hierüber noch mündlichen Vortrag vorbehalten."

15. 16 July 1884. Prince Bismarck, in Varzin, to German foreign office. Cipher telegram. No. 7. Reichsarchiv, Vermischtes Südwestafrika IV.

"Sollte Lord Ampthill inzwischen Note wegen Angra übergeben, so wollen Euere Excellenz ihm vertraulich gleich bemerken dass wir, ebensowenig wie England das thäte, bei Ausübung des Rechts unsere Unterthanen zu schützen uns Bedingungen vorschreiben lassen könnten. Schutz englischer Unterthanen selbstverständlich. Strafkolonie nicht beabsichtigt aber als Bedingung mit Würde einer souveränen Macht nicht verträglich."

VI

THE FINAL NEGOTIATIONS

DURING the next two months, from the middle of July to the middle of September, Prince Bismarck was occupied in filling up the lacunae left by Herbert Bismarck, and in attempting to make the British Government realize the seriousness of his intentions by opposing them diplomatically in the Egyptian question. England's troubles in Egypt were approaching a sort of climax. The financial burdens of the Egyptian Government had been greatly increased by the Sudan campaign and by the award of damages resulting from the burning of Alexandria. The only possible remedy was to change the law of liquidation, and England attempted to do this by calling the powers interested in Egypt to a conference which met at London on 28 June 1884. At this conference the British proposals, including the reduction of interest on the unified debt, the floating of a new loan and the transfer of certain revenues to administrative expenses, were strongly opposed by the French, who were more or less openly supported by Germany. As a result, the conference was wholly unsuccessful, and broke up early in August, leaving the English in just as bad a position as they were before.* Lord Granville, who still failed to appreciate Bismarck's policy of bargaining, could not see what was the matter. He said to Count Münster on 13 July 1884 "that I was unable to understand the position of affairs. His Excellency and Count Herbert Bismarck had both assured me of the favourable disposition of the German Government and had stated that no decision would be come to without reference by the Plenipotentiaries to their respective Governments. But it

* William L. Langer: *European Alliances and Alignments, 1871-1890*, pp. 251-318. See especially pp. 282, 298-99, 301-6.

seemed that the German financial delegate had joined the French Members of the Commission in their opposition to our financial proposals, and although no positive opinion had been taken in the last sitting of the Commission, the tendency of Baron Dehrenthal had been to support objections to some of the most material portions of those proposals." Count Münster replied non-committally that the French were very determined in their view, and that Granville probably exaggerated Bismarck's influence. To this Granville would not agree, and he added "that it was unsatisfactory that while Her Majesty's Government had been left in the dark, the French Government had been confident beforehand of the support of foreign delegates and that their anticipations appeared to be justified by the event."* A few days later, on 21 July, Count Münster told Lord Granville that he had communicated with Bismarck, "who had replied that the feeling in France against Germany was so strong that he did not think it advisable that the German Government should put forward any proposal which was not likely to prove acceptable to M. Ferry."† (Ferry was the prime minister of France.) Bismarck was very clearly opposed to giving England any assistance, and whenever Lord Granville took the matter up with Münster, as he did on several other occasions, he always received the same evasive answers. On 24 July Münster told him that Bismarck had to consider that there was a large amount of Egyptian bonds in German hands. "I asked His Excellency how long this portion of the Egyptian debt had been so held. Count Münster laughed, and said that he had asked the same question of M. Waddington who had also laughed. I observed that if by any chance the Bonds had been recently transferred to German subjects for political objects, it would appear very much as if the German Government and ourselves had been somewhat mystified."‡ On 26 July Ampt-

* 14 July 1884. Lord Granville to Lord Ampthill. No. 204. Draft. F.O. 64/1048.

† 21 July 1884. Lord Granville to Lord Ampthill. No. 212, Confidential. Draft. F.O. 64/1048.

‡ 24 July 1884. Lord Granville to Lord Ampthill. Draft. No. 216, Confidential. F.O. 64/1048.

hill wrote privately to Granville that, according to the Frankfort chamber of commerce, the German bondholders now represented fifteen million pounds sterling of the unified loan (1). This transfer of the Egyptian debt to Frankfort appears to have been carried through by the Rothschilds (2). No further information on the subject is available, but, especially in view of Bismarck's earlier repeated protestations that Germany had no interest whatsoever in Egypt, the suspicion is certainly justified that this sudden transfer of the Egyptian bonds had a political connection. Even after July 1884, Bismarck's language to Münster was always that the Egyptian question was in itself a matter of no importance to Germany, and that it only assumed importance when it became a means of settling the colonial question, which, for reasons of domestic policy and public opinion, was a matter of life and death.

Bismarck's unfriendly policy in the Egyptian conference gave emphasis to the vigorous protest he now made in regard to the condition about a penal settlement. In a despatch to Münster of 24 July 1884 he declared that the recognition of Germany's claims by the British Government excluded the possibility that England could impose conditions on the manner in which Germany was to exercise them. England knew already that he had no intention of establishing a penal settlement, but the demand that Germany should, by giving an assurance to this effect, bind herself in the exercise of her indisputable rights, was unusual, and such an obligation had never been undertaken by England in similar circumstances. Bismarck said he could not recommend the emperor to accept the obligation proposed by England. He added that it was a matter of course that the acquired rights of British subjects in this territory would be respected. He requested Münster to read these instructions to Lord Granville, and to leave him a copy of them.*

On 7 August 1884, Count Münster discussed this matter in some detail with Lord Granville, who said he was surprised

* 24 July 1884. Prince Bismarck to Count Münster. German White Book, *Angra Pequena*, No. 33.

that official objection had been taken "to a note which had been agreed upon between Count Herbert Bismarck and myself." The sentence complained of "did not at the time strike either Count H. Bismarck or myself as objectionable, and I could not help thinking that the objection was not so strong in reality as seemed to be felt by Prince Bismarck. The words used were meant only to imply that we wished to be sure that the assurance which Count H. Bismarck had given me would be confirmed by his Government." But Granville had no wish to retain the phrase. He proposed that England as well as Germany should undertake an obligation not to establish a penal settlement on that coast. If this were not agreeable to Germany, he would be satisfied with a despatch confirming Herbert Bismarck's assurances.* Münster, in his account of this conversation, wrote much the same, and declared that he had impressed upon Lord Granville how earnestly Bismarck looked upon this matter, and how German policy might be influenced by it. He added that Granville had made still another suggestion, that Ampthill's note of 19 July should be returned, and should be altered in conformity with the wishes of the German Government (3).

Thus Lord Granville had substantially withdrawn the condition he had tried to impose on the English recognition of the situation at Angra Pequena. The further suggestions which he made to Münster in the conversation of 7 August were almost as unfortunate as the official note to which Bismarck had objected, but at least they made it clear that Granville was not trying to impose an obligation on the German Government, and that all he wanted was a repetition of the statements that had already been made to him, for the benefit of British public opinion.

On 13 August Bismarck informed the German foreign office that since Ampthill's note of 19 July had already been answered, he did not lay any value on its withdrawal, and desired that no answer should be given to Granville's sug-

* 7 August 1884. Lord Granville to Lord Ampthill. British Blue Book, (C. 4262), No. 2, Enclosure 3.

gestion to this effect (4). But he objected to Granville's statement that his despatch to Lord Ampthill of 14 July had been concerted with Count Herbert Bismarck, and Count Herbert Bismarck himself vigorously denied this assertion when he was informed of it. He said he had received a copy of this despatch from Lord Granville on the evening of 13 July, at the moment of his departure from London, had made no reply whatever, and had sent this copy on to Berlin the next day with certain comments of his own (5). But these comments, which have been described at the end of the last chapter,* attempted to explain that the expression in Granville's despatch regarding a penal settlement was a harmless one, and implied no wish for the German Government to undertake an obligation. In other words, Count Herbert Bismarck regarded the matter much in the same light that Lord Granville did, which would indicate that, even if he had not discussed the exact wording of the despatch in question, he had gone over the subject with Lord Granville and had not impossibly encouraged him in his point of view. This appears to be one of the points where Count Herbert Bismarck was not entirely successful.

But, although this question was now settled, Bismarck soon found other grounds for irritation against the British Government. Lord Derby's telegram to the Cape Colony on 14 July had declared that England could not oppose the German claim to protect the acquisitions of Lüderitz, and that they would henceforth be placed under German protection, but that the British Government were prepared to annex any other territories on that coast that the Cape Colony might desire. But this was not enough for the Cape Parliament which, on 16 July 1884, voted unanimously for the annexation of the whole of the territory between the Orange River and the Portuguese boundary, including the acquisitions of Lüderitz and Angra Pequena. Although the Cape Government were no doubt encouraged by Lord Derby's attitude, this act was in entire contradiction to the statements about German protection which were made in his telegram.

* See pages 107–8.

When this news reached the German foreign office, Hatzfeldt telegraphed to London on 21 July, to ask Münster to inquire whether the instructions to the Cape Colony forbidding any further step in regard to Angra Pequena, which Granville had promised Count Herbert Bismarck should be sent on 17 June, had really been sent and if so on what date.* Münster telegraphed back that they had been sent on 14 July.† There was some confusion here, since the promised instructions to the Cape had really been sent off on 17 June,‡ and Derby's telegram of 14 July had contained a very different message. In any case, Hatzfeldt was not satisfied with the answer from London, for on 26 July he telegraphed to the German consul in Cape Town asking to be informed by telegram of the decision of the Cape Parliament and the wording of Lord Derby's telegram to Cape Town of 14 July.§ The consul telegraphed back on 28 July giving the desired information,|| which was forwarded from Berlin to London on 2 August, with a number of bitter comments on the English manner of proceeding.¶

The question was settled in regard to one part of this territory when on 7 August 1884 the coast line from the Orange River to 26 degrees of south latitude was officially proclaimed to be under German protection by the captain of the German ship *Elizabeth*.** Notification to foreign powers immediately followed, and on 16 August Baron von Plessen, the German chargé d'affaires in London, reported that he had verbally informed the British foreign office of this act.††

* 21 July 1884. Count Hatzfeldt to Count Münster. Telegram. German White Book, *Angra Pequena,* No. 31.

† 22 July 1884. Count Münster to Count Hatzfeldt. Telegram. *Ibid.,* No. 32.

‡ 17 June 1884. Lord Derby to Sir Hercules Robinson. Telegram. British Blue Book, (C. 4190), No. 60.

§ 26 July 1884. Count Hatzfeldt to the German consul in Cape Town. Telegram. German White Book, *Angra Pequena,* No. 34.

|| 28 July 1884. The German consul in Cape Town to Count Hatzfeldt. Telegram. *Ibid.,* No. 35.

¶ 2 August 1884. Count Hatzfeldt to Count Münster. *Ibid.,* No. 36.

** 14 August 1884. Captain of the *Elizabeth* to the imperial admiralty in Berlin. Telegram. *Ibid.,* No. 39.

†† 16 August 1884. Baron von Plessen to German foreign office. Telegram. No. 134. Reichsarchiv, Vermischtes Südwestafrika V.

A further report from the German consul in Cape Town, dated 23 July 1884, reached the foreign office in Berlin on 15 August. This gave the details of the discussion in the Cape Parliament, and related how the government had at first proposed to annex only the coast between the Cape Colony and Walfisch Bay, and how an amendment was unanimously adopted making the annexation extend all the way up to the southern boundary of the Portuguese colony.† A telegram was now, on 17 August, addressed to the German chargé d'affaires in London, asking him to inform the British foreign office that the decision of the Cape Colony had embarrassed the German Government, since they had made exactly the same decision themselves.‡ To this communication Sir Julian Pauncefote replied, on 18 August, that so far as he knew the Cape Colony had only annexed that territory which lay outside the German claims. In any case their annexation was not yet carried out. He did not believe this question would lead to any further difficulties, and promised to give a fuller answer as soon as it was possible.§

Lord Granville was "disposed to think that no objection can properly be taken to the action of the German Government in this matter," but considered that inquiry should be made as to the nature of the protection referred to by Germany. He suggested to Lord Derby "that the Cape Government be informed by telegraph of the communication made by the German Government, and be cautioned against interfering with the claims of Germany between the Orange River and the 26th degree of south latitude."|| It is clear that Lord Granville's first wish was now to settle with the German Government, and that he was in no mood for concessions to the Cape Colony which might endanger this settlement. But he did not understand the full significance of

† 23 July 1884. The German consul in Cape Town to Prince Bismarck. German White Book, *Angra Pequena,* No. 38.

‡ 17 August 1884. Count Hatzfeldt to Baron von Plessen. Telegram. *Ibid.,* No. 40.

§ 18 August 1884. Baron von Plessen to Prince Bismarck. *Ibid.,* No. 43.

|| 20 August 1884. Foreign office to colonial office. British Blue Book, (C. 4262), No. 5.

Plessen's communication, which was that the German Government had made *exactly* the same decision as the Cape Government, and intended to annex the *entire* coast themselves. Lord Granville appears to have thought that all that Bismarck objected to was the attempt of the Cape Colony to annex that part of the coast which had already been placed under German protection, from the Orange River to 26 degrees of south latitude, and he did not realize that Germany wanted the whole coast.

This error was very soon cleared up when, on 19 August 1884, Hatzfeldt instructed Plessen to inform Lord Granville that north of the acquisitions of Lüderitz German subjects had acquired rights by treaty with the independent native chieftains, and had asked for German protection. The German Government was disposed to grant this protection, since the treaties were in order and the rights of third parties were not affected. It was for this reason that Germany was embarrassed by the claim put forward by the Cape Colony to territories on the southwest coast of Africa which were outside of British jurisdiction. This claim was in conflict with the public statement as to the limits of British jurisdiction in Africa which was made in 1880, and the German Government could not have expected that their inquiry as to the British title would lead to an endeavor to extend British jurisdiction in competition with German enterprises.* This communication was made by Baron von Plessen to the British foreign office on 22 August.†

A further statement of the German views was made on 26 August 1884, when Plessen, by direction of his government, handed in to the British foreign office a note which formally demanded that the British Government should refuse to sanction the decision of the Cape Parliament. This note recapitulated the history of the negotiations, expressed surprise that the British Government should act contrary to their offi-

* 19 August 1881. Count Hatzfeldt to Baron von Plessen. German White Book, *Angra Pequena*, No. 41.

† 28 August 1884. Foreign office to colonial office. British Blue Book, (C. 4262), No. 9.

cial declarations of 1880, and accused Lord Derby of directly inspiring the action of the Cape Colony by his telegram of 14 July.*

On 23 August 1884 Bismarck gave orders that the German flag should be hoisted over the territories near Walfisch Bay that had been acquired by the Hansemann-Bleichröder Dyes Company. He did not, he said, wish further instructions to be given in this line, until he had heard what reply would be made to the latest representations of Baron von Plessen in London, for if England ignored his request in regard to the decision of the Cape Parliament, he intended to make a complete break with her. The object was too trifling to be a cause of war, but he would attempt to create diplomatic difficulties for England on every side, and, as a natural consequence of this, attempt to come to a closer understanding with France.† Meanwhile the question was being played up in the German newspapers, and Lord Derby's communications to the Cape Colony, which had been published in Cape Town, were reproduced in the official *Norddeutsche Allgemeine Zeitung*. "The feeling in Germany respecting these Colonial Questions is so strong," wrote Lord Ampthill on 18 August, a week before his death, "that the publication of the above-named correspondence can only tend to confirm the General suspicion that England opposes the Colonial Aspirations of the people of Germany, and the impression of disappointment it must produce will be painful and lasting throughout Germany."‡

How seriously Bismarck really took the decision of the Cape Parliament, it is impossible to say. On 12 August 1884 he criticized Münster very severely for not making the German demands clear to England, and thereby endangering the good relations between the two countries, which he had

* 22 August 1884. Count Hatzfeldt to Baron von Plessen, sending a plan for a note to Lord Granville. German White Book, *Angra Pequena*, No. 42. This note was handed in by Plessen on 26 August, and appears in British Blue Book, (C. 4262), No. 10, Enclosure 1.

† 23 August 1884. Memorandum by Count Wilhelm Bismarck in Varzin. *Die Grosse Politik*, IV, No. 750.

‡ 18 August 1884. Lord Ampthill to Lord Granville. No. 225. F.O. 64/1103.

wished to maintain.* But Ampthill thought Bismarck was deliberately exciting the press against England for the sole purpose of increasing his own popularity by taking advantage of the national craze (6). And certainly it is difficult to see why the resolution of the Cape Parliament, which had not yet been carried out and was not likely to be for some time, should be sufficient ground for a complete break with England. Münster, also, looked upon the tone of the press as nothing more than a Parliamentary maneuver. He wrote privately to Granville from Germany: "All will change after the elections: thunderclouds come and go."†

In any case, Bismarck had no occasion to put his threats into effect, for the British Government backed down. The tone of the German press and the reports of Lord Ampthill made abundantly clear the line Bismarck was taking. The situation was further clarified when, at the end of August, the rest of the coast of South West Africa, from 26 degrees of south latitude to Cape Frio, was placed under German protection. News of this reached the German foreign office in a telegram from Cape Town dated 5 September 1884,‡ and the chargé d'affaires in London was immediately instructed to inform the British Government,§ which he did on 8 September, proposing at the same time that the final settlement of the question should be entrusted to commissioners to be named for the purpose.||

The British reply was a note handed in by the British chargé d'affaires at Berlin on 22 September. This note stated that "if, as Her Majesty's Government gather from the information now before them, it is the intention of Germany

* 12 August 1884. Prince Bismarck to Count Münster. *Die Grosse Politik,* No. 749.

† 25 August 1884. Count Münster to Lord Granville. Private. Lord Edmond Fitzmaurice: *Life of Lord Granville,* II, 359.

‡ 5 September 1884. German consul in Cape Town to German foreign office. Telegram. German White Book, *Angra Pequena,* No. 46.

§ 7 September 1884. Busch to German chargé d'affaires in London. Telegram. *Ibid.,* No. 47.

|| 13 September 1884. Lord Granville to British chargé d'affaires in Berlin. British Blue Book, (C. 4262), No. 14, Enclosure.

to establish in the region described a Colony or territorial political protectorate of a defined type, Her Majesty's Government will welcome Germany as a neighbour on those parts of the coast which are not already within the limits of the Cape Colony, and not actually in British possession."* This answer had the effect of satisfying Bismarck at last, and Baron von Plessen informed the British foreign office that Bismarck observed that he saw in the British note a first step in that direction which he had hoped British policy would take, "and added that he could have wished in the interests of the present and the future that it had been taken earlier."†

There still remained a number of lesser points to settle. There were disputes between the English traders and Lüderitz, in regard to their respective claims on the mainland, and in regard to one of the islands in the Bay of Angra Pequena. But these differences were too small to form the subject of any further diplomatic friction. Suggestions had already been made on both sides that the final details might be submitted to a mixed commission, and on 19 September 1884 the English chargé d'affaires in Berlin informed the German foreign office that the British Government would be ready to agree to such an arrangement.‡ The German assent to this proposal was given in a note to the British foreign office of 8 October 1884,§ and the commission met at Cape Town during the months March to September 1885, and produced their findings at the end of that year.||

* 22 September 1884. The British chargé d'affaires in Berlin to Count Hatzfeldt. British Blue Book, (C. 4262), No. 42, Enclosure.

† 29 September 1884. Lord Granville to British chargé d'affaires in Berlin. *Ibid.*, No. 32, Enclosure. The words in quotation marks were omitted from the Blue Book. Full version in F.O. 64/1103.

‡ 19 September 1884. The British chargé d'affaires in Berlin to Lord Granville. British Blue Book, (C. 4262), No. 31, Enclosure.

§ 6 October 1884. Busch to Plessen, sending a plan for a note to Lord Granville. German White Book, *Angra Pequena,* No. 50. The note was handed in on 8 October 1884, as reported in a despatch from Plessen to Bismarck on that date. *Ibid.*, No. 51.

|| *Proceedings of the Angra Pequena and West Coast Claims Joint Commission, March-September, 1885.* Printed at Cape Town, 1885. A copy of this is to be found in F.O. 64/1106.

NOTES

1. 26 July 1884. Lord Ampthill to Lord Granville. Private. Private Granville MSS, G.D. 29/178.

"They [the diplomats] all, have come round to the impression that the German Government, with a view to popularity in the coming general election, wish it to appear that they have protected the interests of the German Bondholders, who, according to the Frankfort Chamber of Commerce, represent fifteen million Pound Sterling of the Unified Loan, against the proposed ½% reduction of interest."

2. 26 November 1884. Lord Granville to Sir Edward Malet. Draft. Private. Private Granville MSS, G.D. 29/206.

"Germany has an interest [in Egypt], since the Rothschilds transferred so large an amount of Egyptian debt to Frankfort."

3. 8 August 1884. Count Münster to Prince Bismarck. German White Book, *Angra Pequena,* No. 37. Full version in Reichsarchiv, Vermischtes Südwestafrika V. The following paragraph was omitted from the White Book:

". . . Soeben sah ich Lord Granville wieder und er sagte mir, dass er nach näherer Ueberlegung glaube, dass es am Besten sein würde, wenn Lord Ampthill seine Note zurückfordere und sie dann eine andere Fassung bekäme, die dann zu vereinbaren wäre."

4. 13 August 1884. Count Wilhelm Bismarck, in Varzin, to German foreign office. Reichsarchiv, Vermischtes Südwestafrika V.

". . . Da die Note von Lord Granville vom 19. v.M. von uns bereits beantwortet worden ist, so ist deren Zurückziehung dem Reichskanzler nicht mehr von Werth, und er wünscht, dass auch bezüglich dieses Punktes unsre schweigende Haltung bezüglich Angra Pequena nicht alterirt werde. Eine Erwiederung auf das Granville'schen Anerbieten, die Note vom 19. v.M. zurückzuziehen, werde danach zu unterlassen sein."

5. 11 August 1884. Extract from a private letter from Count Herbert Bismarck, in Königstein, enclosed in Count Wilhelm Bismarck's letter to the German foreign office of 13 August 1884. Reichsarchiv, Vermischtes Südwestafrika V.

"Es ist eine Unwahrheit, wenn Granville behauptet, mit mir über seinen letzten Erlass an Ampthill, von dem dieser die Note vom 19. v.M. einfach abgeschrieben hat, vorher gesprochen zu haben. Ich erhielt einen kurzen Privatbrief Granville's mit der Abschrift des Erlasses an Ampthill am Abend des 13. Juli im Momente meiner Abreise, antwortete *garnichts* darauf und schickte die Sachen vom Haag aus mittelst eines Berichts vom 14. v.M. ein, in welchem ich auf das Anfassende des Wortes 'security' against a penal settlement aufmerksam machte.

"Möglicherweise hat Gr. Münster Granville auch noch missverstanden. Ich vermuthe das nach der Angabe Gf. Münster's, dass 'der Text der Note mit mir vereinbart worden wäre.' Darauf würde ich mich ja niemals eingelassen haben. Granville hat mir seinen Erlass an Ampthill ohne jede Vorbereitung zugeschickt, *nachdem* er an Ampthill expedirt worden war."

6. 16 August 1884. Lord Ampthill to Lord Granville. Private. Private Granville MSS, G.D. 29/178.

". . . Of course Bismarck knows what he is about and he is taking advantage of the national craze that England opposes Germany's Colonial Aspirations, as an election cry, which may finally secure him the working majority in the coming elections, he had bid for in vain in the two former general elections to the Reichstag."

VII

CONCLUSION

BISMARCK'S displeasure was by no means ended by the settlement that had been reached in regard to Angra Pequena. He continued to express his resentment at the way he thought England had treated him, and his attitude towards England in diplomatic affairs remained for some further time unfriendly. On 19 October 1884 Count Münster, just back from two months' leave in Germany, told Granville that "Prince Bismarck had felt himself aggrieved by our [England's] conduct in the Angra Pequena affair, though he hoped that question might be considered as good as settled."* On 5 December 1884 Sir Edward Malet, the new ambassador to Berlin, wrote that he felt "in some dismay as to the ultimate intentions of the Chancellor. You will have gathered from the reports which I have sent you, that his general tone towards us is neither cordial nor friendly. . . ."† Later, in January 1885, Bismarck told Malet that England's failure to coöperate with him on the colonial question had forced him to seek the fulfillment of his wishes by means of an understanding with France. He "parenthetically remarked that he could not maintain Count Münster as Ambassador in London," since he had failed to make clear the importance attached to the colonial question. Bismarck at the same time read Malet a despatch he was about to send to Münster which, Malet reported, "is one which I should say was designed to cause Count Münster to resign." (Münster was in fact transferred to Paris late in 1885.) Malet added: "The general impression which I derived from the conversation was that the Prince

* 19 October 1884. Lord Granville to Sir Edward Malet. Africa No. 39B. F.O. 244/384.

† 5 December 1884. Sir Edward Malet to Lord Granville. Private. Private Granville MSS, G.D. 29/179.

does not desire that relations between the two countries should improve at present."*

Even after the Angra Pequena settlement the German press continued hostile to England, and this hostility was further stimulated when, on 11 December 1884, Bismarck laid before the Reichstag a White Book containing documents which covered the whole history of the negotiations. This publication, which was fully described in the British press, made an unfavorable impression on British public opinion as well. The appearance of three British Blue Books on the same subject, two of them of enormous size, did little to alter this impression. "The broad facts of the case are, we regret to say, beyond dispute," wrote *The Times,* and added that in none of the numerous and lengthy documents which had been published "have we been able to find any satisfactory defence of the manner in which the business of the nation is conducted by the most highly placed and most thoroughly trusted Ministers of the Crown." It might be possible, said *The Times,* to show that German diplomacy had not been quite so straight-forward and single-minded as the White Book made it appear. "But the material issues are unaffected by any slight corrections of this nature, which it would now be as unbecoming as it would be unavailing to press against the German Government."†

The view of *The Times* was shared by several members of the British cabinet. Chamberlain told Count Herbert Bismarck, on 24 September 1884: "It is absolutely mad of English foreign policy unnecessarily to provoke Germany, with whom we could so easily be good friends."‡ Dilke felt much the same. On 4 October 1884, he said to Herbert Bismarck: "I cannot tell you how deeply I regret the perverseness and lack of skill in our policy towards you in Colonial matters.

* 24 January 1885. Sir Edward Malet to Lord Granville. British Blue Book, (C. 4273), No. 148a. Words here quoted omitted from Blue Book but appear in original in F.O. 64/1146.

† *The Times:* 24 December 1884, p. 7, col. 2.

‡ 24 September 1884. Memorandum by Count Herbert Bismarck. *Die Grosse Politik,* IV, No. 753.

You had every right to complain about our silly attitude. The wrong was on our side. I will offer no word of excuse, for none is possible. You had explained to us with the greatest frankness the claims and the course of your policy, and it is unheard of that Lord Granville did not meet your wishes."* In March 1885 Lord Hartington declared frankly to Count Herbert Bismarck "that the inclusion of Lord Derby in the cabinet had been a mistake: he expressed his regret at the latter's secretive behaviour, and attributed to him the major responsibility for our 'misunderstandings.' "†

But the rights of the matter were not in any case so clear as this, and, while the British Government may have been partially to blame, there were other reasons for the "misunderstandings." The mistakes made by Count Münster undoubtedly played a large part in the negotiations at cross purposes which went on between the two governments, and long after the Angra Pequena question was closed Bismarck continued to upbraid him and to assert that by his failure to make things clear to the British Government he was the chief cause of the quarrel.‡ But his criticism was always that Münster had not placed before the British Government the alternatives of maintaining a friendly attitude towards German colonies or of losing German support in Egypt. It is quite true that Münster had failed to do this effectively, but this was not the real cause of the dispute. The leading British ministers, with the exception of Lord Derby, were not particularly inclined to oppose German colonization in any case, and were prepared to grant Bismarck's wishes when they understood them. The reason they did not understand his wishes was that they were never informed of them, by Münster or anyone else. Up to the middle of June 1884 Münster never told Granville that Germany wanted to found a

* 5 October 1884. Memorandum by Count Herbert Bismarck. E.T.S. Dugdale: *German Diplomatic Documents, 1871-1914,* I, 186.

† 7 March 1885. Count Herbert Bismarck to Prince Bismarck. *Die Grosse Politik,* IV, No. 760.

‡ Prince Bismarck to Count Münster: 24 January, 25 January, 3 February, 1885. *Die Grosse Politik,* IV, Nos. 757, 758, 759.

colony at Angra Pequena, and he was never criticized by Bismarck for this omission. Münster in fact could not make such a communication, for he was incompletely informed himself and did not understand what was happening. He was merely an instrument.

It is clear that Bismarck did not act deceptively at the beginning of the negotiations, for at that time he had probably not decided on a colonial policy. But when he changed his plans he made no effort to inform the British Government, and his earlier communications thus served in effect as a screen for his intentions. Of particular interest is Bismarck's use of the word "protection." With considerable skill, he avoided defining it throughout the entire course of the negotiations. At the time of his first inquiry he left the impression that this term as used by him definitely did not connote annexation. Hence the British Government failed to realize what he was about when he indicated he might extend protection or when he actually did so. Later he explained to England that the possibility of a British annexation had now been excluded, and when England expressed surprise at this situation, Bismarck pointed to his announcement of "protection." The meaning he attached to this ambiguous word changed in the course of time, but this change was never explained to England. It is certain that Bismarck deliberately kept Münster incompletely informed, it is certain also that he expected opposition to his projects from the English side, and in view of the whole history of the negotiations he can hardly be absolved from the charge of seeking to further his aims by concealing them from the British Government.

It appears that Bismarck was quite correct in anticipating English opposition. The proposal of the colonists to annex Angra Pequena and Lord Derby's actions in their support show this beyond a doubt, although Derby's weakness toward colonial demands did not extend to the rest of the cabinet. However, even if Bismarck had declared his intentions from the first, his position in Europe was so impregnable that the British Government could hardly have opposed him had they wanted to. And probably no member of the cabinet but Lord Derby would have wanted to. Bismarck by his secrecy made it possible for England to consider taking Angra Pequena herself and furnished her with the excuse that she had not been informed of his intentions. Later, when it appeared that England might come to the point of making an annexation, he found it necessary to resort to fuller explanations and even threats to stop her. This was one cause of the dispute, and had Bismarck acted otherwise it might have been avoided.

But the fact that a dispute occurred over Angra Pequena was by no means wholly due to Bismarck. The mistakes of the British Government played a large part. For if, at the beginning of the negotiations, England had returned a frank reply to Bismarck's question about her title, if she had immediately admitted that she had none, Bismarck would have been spared his later pains to make her acquiesce in his position. It was perfectly well known to the British Government that they had no claims or jurisdiction on the mainland at Angra Pequena and, as related in Chapter II, they were on the point of saying so to Bismarck when Scanlen, prime minister of the Cape Colony, intervened. The preposterous claim to exclude other powers from the mainland which England then put forward was due almost wholly to Lord Derby's susceptibility to the representations of the colonists. Derby realized the extraordinary part he had played in the negotiations and wrote to Gladstone after the whole affair was over, hoping that the sole responsibility for what had been done in the colonial question might not be thrown on him. He wanted it to be publicly understood, he said, that the acts of the British Government were the result of their deliberations in common (1). But this line of defense is hardly tenable. Whether Derby should have had the lead or not, there is no doubt that in fact he did have it and that the policy of the British Government in regard to Angra Pequena, up to June 1884, was his policy. His wishes were carried out by the foreign office and he was in effect directly responsible for the conduct of the British side of the negotiations. He prevented a satisfactory reply from being given to Bismarck's clearly stated question, and in his desire to gratify the Cape Colony he pursued a policy which got his country into severe international difficulties.

Of course Derby should never have been allowed to exercise such authority. In handing over the whole responsibility to the colonial office Lord Granville was slack and careless. He seems to have thought that this was a question of minor importance which could safely be left entirely to the discretion of the colonial office and the Cape Colony. Granville had the reputation of trusting subordinates in matters of detail while conducting the negotiations himself, and it was also his practice, as the Duke of Argyll wrote, to consult his colleagues at every step, so that his conduct of the foreign office was never personal or departmental, but rested upon the responsibility of the cabinet.* In this case Granville carried rather too far his practice of consulting the colonial office, while he apparently did not consult the other cabinet members at all. He was by no means a stupid man, nor was he ordinarily slow to take a hint. But he was old and in bad health, and Bismarck's sudden and unannounced colonial departure created an unprecedented situation. In any case, Granville's failure to take alarm and to develop a coherent and effective British policy had unfortunate repercussions on the last years of his career. He was attacked by the press as the one most responsible for what were popularly considered reverses in foreign policy during the Liberal administration in the German colonial question, the Majuba crisis, and the Gordon incident. This disapproval was shared by a number of political leaders, and Gladstone, when he attempted to form a cabinet in January 1886, found a strong feeling "amongst all those he had consulted, that it would have been impossible for Lord Granville to have returned to the Foreign Office; besides, no one of his age had ever been Foreign Secretary." It had been, he told the Queen, "a most painful busi-

* 15 April 1891. Duke of Argyll to Editor of *The Times*. *The Times*, 16 April 1891, p. 10, col. 3.

EARL GRANVILLE

ness."* Ultimately Lord Granville, in spite of his protest that taking a lower office would injure his position as leader of the Liberal party in the House of Lords, was induced to accept the colonial office in the ministry of 1886, and after it went out, in June of that year, he never held office again. Even the Duke of Argyll, who warmly supported Granville and felt he had been unjustly blamed for mistakes committed by the cabinet as a whole, was inclined to hold him responsible in the German colonial question. "The only faults," Argyll wrote to Granville, "which seemed to me to be possibly *departmental* only were those connected with the new colonial policy of the Germans, in which it seemed as if you had not taken alarm in time, or replied in time to certain despatches. Probably you have a good explanation; but whether you have or not, it is not on this that the public feeling has been adverse, but on the policy in Egypt etc. . . ."†

At the end of the negotiations the British Government stood in a curious position. Its principal leaders were averse to further colonial expansion, and were fully occupied in any case by their difficulties in Egypt and by domestic problems. Yet England was placed in the apparent situation of trying to obtain South West Africa, a territory she had previously refused to appropriate, and yielding reluctantly to the German claims. This situation was only apparent, for it must be remembered that no proposal to annex Angra Pequena was ever laid before the British cabinet until the Cape Government voted for this measure on 16 July 1884. By that time England had accepted the German position, and she turned down the Cape proposal. The British cabinet never attempted to annex Angra Pequena, no matter what may have been the wishes of Derby and the Cape Parliament. Bismarck's protests were directed against the actions of Derby and the Cape, never against the official British policy. The situation was tangled, because of the loose connection in questions of foreign af-

* 1 February 1886. Extract from the Queen's Journal. G. E. Buckle: *Letters of Queen Victoria*, 3rd Series, I, 35.

† 11 February 1886. Duke of Argyll to Lord Granville. Lord Edmond Fitzmaurice: *Life of Lord Granville,* II, 480.

fairs between the foreign office, the colonial office, and the Cape Colony. This resulted in a free hand for Derby who, unaware of the seriousness of Bismarck's intentions and influenced mainly by the pressure of public opinion, both English and colonial, tried unsuccessfully to bring the sentiment of the Cape Colony up to annexation point before a German action took place.

Looking at the situation from the standpoint of immediate advantages in international politics, the British policy was a most unfortunate one. It accomplished nothing beneficial to England, and resulted only in the estrangement of the most powerful government in Europe, which meant for some time to come a heavy additional burden on England in her Egyptian troubles. On the other hand it does not appear that the British Government sacrificed any valuable English interests. A new rival had indeed entered the colonial field. But the German acquisitions, in South West Africa and elsewhere, were neither so valuable nor so large as seriously to endanger British colonial supremacy. To England German colonization was a matter of secondary interest, and Gladstone and Granville realized this and acted accordingly when the situation finally became clarified. The British policy showed a lack of effective leadership, it was clumsy and muddled, but the charge cannot be made that the interests of the English people were not adequately safeguarded.

The Egyptian question was crucial. The senior English ministers were not anxious for new annexations and were convinced that opposition to German colonization would serve no real British interest, but the immediate reason for their backing down was that Bismarck had begun to exert pressure in Egypt. What made the Egyptian question so important was the grouping of the powers after the British occupation in 1882. This occupation had ended the Anglo-French entente under which affairs in Egypt had previously been regulated. Thus France and England, once friendly, were now opposed, and each had to make her own terms with Bismarck and his eastern group of powers, whose relative strength was doubled by the division of the other side. Bismarck was thus in a strong position, which was made almost impregnable by the entente with France, which began in 1884 and lasted until the fall of Jules Ferry in 1885.

The Franco-German entente meant that Bismarck was prepared to support France against England in the Egyptian question, an arrangement that placed England in an almost untenable position and forced her to give in to Bismarck's demands. The entente was important for one other reason. The question of naval supremacy never emerged into the foreground during the colonial dispute, but it nevertheless played a significant, if hidden, part. There was of course never any danger of war between Germany and England at this time. Gladstone and his colleagues saw clearly that the German colonial question was not worth fighting about, and British public opinion, had it been consulted, would no doubt have taken the same line. Bismarck, while he was prepared for a break with England, has made it perfectly clear that he had no intention of pushing matters to the point of war. But no great power can act without consideration of the possibility of war. Hence it was a fact of the greatest importance that while England possessed what was numerically the strongest navy in the world, she would have been outnumbered by the combined fleets of the powers, including France, that were grouped around Bismarck at the moment. This is not to say that England could have been beaten by such a combination, or even that such a combination was likely to occur. It was the possibility, not the actuality, of naval cooperation between the continental powers that offset England's naval superiority and made her helpless to oppose the German claims.

These conclusions may be summed up as follows: (i) Bismarck's first communication regarding South West Africa, in February 1883, was so worded as to give the impression, correct at that time, that he on no account wished to acquire colonies. This impression was never contradicted, and Bismarck made no attempt to explain the change in his plans when this change took place. The additional fact that passages in which he explicitly disclaimed a colonial policy were omitted from the White Book supports the conclusion that he was using his earlier statements to conceal his objectives. (ii) It is quite clear that the blunders of Münster greatly increased the misunderstanding. The fact that there was excuse for some of these blunders strengthens the case against Bismarck. (iii) The British foreign office was the legal organ for negotiating with Bismarck, but in practice it was greatly influenced both by the colonial office and by the Government of the Cape Colony. This triple control led to slow action and an inconsistent foreign policy on the British side, a policy which not only failed to accomplish anything but also brought the British Government into a very uncomfortable international situation. (iv) There is no evidence to show that the British Government tried to deceive or overreach Bismarck. They were convinced that Bismarck did not desire colonial possessions and would agree to a British annexation of Angra Pequena. For this delusion they were not entirely to blame. Their misconception cannot, however, excuse them for failing either to understand or to answer Bismarck's question regarding their title to Angra Pequena. (v) The British policy, though it resulted in diplomatic defeat, did not entail the loss of any important British interests in the long run. The leaders of the British Government realized this and for that reason were the more ready to give way to Bismarck's demands. (vi) There was at no time any danger that the dispute would lead to war. Neither country desired it, and England was not in a position to fight even if she had wished to. Bismarck saw this and, realizing the strength of his position, made full use of his special advantages.

It is very unlikely that a formal naval alliance of the continental powers against England could have been brought about. The Franco-German understanding was altogether too loose and temporary an affair to afford basis for such action. It could not in the nature of things long endure, for it depended on the continuation of the policy of Ferry, and Ferry was sharply watched by a jealous opposition. It has been well said that Bismarck's diplomatic experiment was built on the quicksand of French public opinion. Of course Bismarck was quite aware of this, and by the time Ferry was overthrown he was well on the way to a reconciliation with England, and was ready to proceed in combination with her. By that time he had achieved his main objects anyway. During the first year of the German colonial program he had fully profited by his opportunities. With a diplomacy as adroit as that of his opponents was clumsy he had secured large oversea territories which, even if they were not of great value, were at any rate inexpensively acquired. The time was propitious for a German colonial policy, and once Bismarck had determined on this objective Franco-British hostility in Egypt assured his success.

NOTE

1. 15 January 1885. Lord Derby to Mr. Gladstone. Private. Private Gladstone MSS.

"I thank you for your letter. The newspaper outcry about colonial affairs does not trouble me: it comes too early to affect the elections of next year, and other subjects will soon cause it to be forgotten. Only this I hope I may claim—that the Cabinet whose views I have followed all along, will not throw or allow to be thrown the sole responsibility of what has been done or left undone, on me. The opposition will from obvious reasons be well inclined to do so: and probably the more radical section of the party also. . . . I am ready to answer for all our acts, but I do wish it to be understood that they are not exclusively or specially mine, but the result of our deliberations in common."

APPENDIX I

JOSEPH CHAMBERLAIN AND THE MAJUBA CRISIS

CHAMBERLAIN'S utterances on the retrocession of the Transvaal at the time of the Majuba crisis in 1881 throw an interesting light on the early views of one who is commonly supposed to have been a strong imperialist all his life. He objected to the annexation of the Transvaal at the time it was made, in 1877; he favored its reversal when the liberal government came into office in 1880; and in 1881, when the government's hand was forced by the conflict at Majuba, and the Boers of the Transvaal were granted a large amount of independence, he vigorously defended the official policy, both in the House of Commons and in public.

There is no doubt that Chamberlain was sincere in his dislike of the annexation of the Transvaal, and that he was not merely forcing himself to take this line because of political expediency. He voted against this annexation when it came up in the House of Commons in 1877,* and had wished for its reversal long before the Majuba incident took place. On coming into office in 1880, he wrote a minute on the subject to Mr. Gladstone: "I doubt the wisdom and the permanence of the annexation. Unless some unforeseen circumstances lead to a large immigration of Englishmen into the Transvaal, I believe the Boers will, sooner or later, worry this country into granting their independence."† He had been asked, in 1880, to act as the spokesman of the cabinet on colonial questions in the House of Commons,‡ and in August of that year it fell to him to defend the maintenance of the annexation in a debate. But even then he declared: "He thought there was not a single Member of the Government who did not regret the annexation of the Transvaal and the time and way in which it

* Henry W. Lucy: *Speeches of Joseph Chamberlain,* p. 19.

† 9 June 1880. Minute by Joseph Chamberlain. J. L. Garvin: *Life of Chamberlain,* I, 439.

‡ *Ibid.,* I, 440.

took place. . . . He might go further, and say the Members of the Government would wish it were possible they could recommend that this country should be now relieved of the responsibility of that act."* And in 1881, a week before Colley's first repulse at Laing's Nek, Chamberlain broke away from the policy the government were pursuing. He refused to vote against a private member's motion condemning the annexation, and walked out.†

When the government decided to restore to the Transvaal its independence, Chamberlain was warm in his defense of their policy. As far as his real reasons for taking this line are shown by his public utterances, he was not thinking about the question of imperialism at all. Only once did he hint at it, when he intimated that the Transvaal was relatively of very little importance: "And if we let them go, this population of 40,000 . . . why this dismembered Empire of ours will still contain 250,000,000 of subjects to the Queen, to rule whom well and wisely is a duty and a responsibility which I think is sufficient even for the wildest ambition."‡

But, except for this one instance, Chamberlain did not at the time touch even remotely on the subject of imperialism, but based his plea on the special circumstances of the case, and tried to show that the retention of the Transvaal was contrary both to the interests and the honor of England. To maintain the annexation, he argued in the House of Commons, was not worth the trouble and expense it would entail. It would have been impossible to keep control over the Transvaal, and, at the same time, to have given free representative local institutions. A despotic government would, therefore, have been necessary, and that would have necessitated the keeping of a large force constantly in South Africa. The re-conquest of the territory did not present insuperable difficulties, although it might have unpleasant consequences in the opposition of the Free State and the agitation of the Dutch in the Cape Colony. "But the enterprise would have been absolutely Quixotic. They would have had permanently to maintain a large army on a European scale. They would have

* 31 August 1880. *Hansard Parliamentary Debates,* CCLVI, 906.

† J. L. Garvin: *Life of Chamberlain,* I, 440.

‡ 7 June 1881. Speech by Chamberlain at Birmingham. Henry W. Lucy: *Speeches of Joseph Chamberlain,* p. 18.

had to risk the best interests of South Africa, and face an insurrection at any moment, when any considerable portion of our troops were removed, and they would have done all this for the purpose of maintaining the supremacy of the Crown over a population of only 40,000 White inhabitants, who were apparently so poor that the utmost revenue that this country could expect from them would not exceed £100,000 per annum."

But Chamberlain insisted that even more important than the question of England's interests was the question of England's honor. When the Transvaal was annexed, it was clearly understood that this was the wish of the Boer inhabitants. Lord Carnarvon had said that the large majority of the population was in favor of the annexation, "and," Chamberlain went on, "that if it were not so he had no desire to take over an unwilling population. . . . It was upon the assumption that the majority of the Boers were in favor of annexation that Parliament consented to it in 1877. If they found out subsequently that the wishes and sentiments of the Boers were entirely misunderstood—that they had gained the Transvaal on false pretences—they were bound in honor to withdraw from the position which they had unwittingly and wrongly taken up." He submitted that as soon as the government became aware of the true feeling of the Boers, as soon as it became manifest that to conciliate them with any offer short of absolute independence was impossible, then "the restoration of their independence was absolutely called for by regard to our Treaty engagements and the honour of our country." In these circumstances, to have continued to maintain the annexation would have been what he could only describe as an act of "force, fraud, and folly."*

Although there can be no question that Chamberlain was thoroughly opposed to the annexation of the Transvaal, it is not certain how far the above statements give the real reasons for his opinion. In a difficult and pressing controversy of this kind, it was only to be expected that Chamberlain would use the arguments most likely to have an effect, rather than the arguments that were most convincing to him personally. He may have been quite sincere when he said that it was contrary to England's honor to maintain the annexation, now that it was known that the Boers

* 25 July 1881. *Hansard Parliamentary Debates,* CCLXIII, 1816-18, 1830-31.

did not want it. But it seems unlikely that this was the reason which weighed with him most, because, in 1877, when it was believed that the Boers were in favor of the annexation, Chamberlain voted against it. And when the liberal government assumed office in 1880, and evidence was still coming in to the effect that the Boers were satisfied, Chamberlain (according to Garvin in the very first meetings of the cabinet) urged the government to revoke the annexation.*

Nor can his real reason for disapproval have been that the Transvaal was worthless to England. What he argued, after the retrocession had been decided upon, was not that the Transvaal was valueless, but that its value was too small to repay the keeping of it by force. The implication left by this argument was that, if the Boers had not opposed the annexation, the Transvaal would have had some value for England, even though a small one, and would therefore have been worth keeping if the Boers agreed. But Chamberlain objected to the annexation even before it had become known that the Boers were dissatisfied.

Some other explanation seems necessary, and we get a strong hint of such an explanation from Chamberlain's political views as a whole, and their influence upon his later conception of empire. It must be remembered that, except for speaking upon colonial matters occasionally in the House, and this did not amount to very much, Chamberlain had very little to do directly with colonies during the second Gladstone administration. Before he took office in 1880, his interest had been centered on questions of domestic policy, and his official position as President of the Board of Trade helped to maintain this direction of his thoughts. He had not had the occasion to give his attention much to colonial matters, and it was only natural that he should have permitted his colonial views to be influenced by his political views.

That he did allow his colonial views to be so influenced is apparent from his statements in later years. He was never, like Lord Rosebery, interested in an empire for the sake of the power and the glory it conferred on England, or for the sake of the material advantages which it afforded. He was fundamentally opposed to the old conception of colonies, that they were "possessions valuable in proportion to the pecuniary advantages

* J. L. Garvin: *Life of Chamberlain,* I, 439.

which they brought to the mother country." He disliked equally the opposite extreme, to which public opinion had drifted after the American Revolution had destroyed this illusion, and when, "because the colonies were no longer a source of revenue, it seems to have been believed and argued by many people that their separation from us was only a matter of time, and that that separation should be desired and encouraged lest haply they might prove an encumbrance and a source of weakness."

Chamberlain never cared about colonies solely because of their commercial value. The thing that touched his imagination was the idea of a system of British democracies all over the world. His ideal was a political union on a sort of radical-democracy basis. A radical himself, he liked the colonies because they were radical too. It was characteristic of him that he omitted India from his scheme for imperial preference.

He scorned the idea that colonies should be regarded as material possessions, or as dependencies. In describing the "true" conception of empire, he said: "The sense of possession has given place to the sentiment of kinship. We think and speak of them as part of ourselves, as part of the British Empire, united to us, although they may be dispersed throughout the world, by ties of kindred, of religion, of history, and of language, and joined to us by the seas that formerly seemed to divide us."*

Chamberlain's later colonial opinions are, therefore, not inconsistent with his early opposition to the annexation of the Transvaal. The idea of annexing a country and keeping it against its will in political subordination was always repugnant to him. He was not insensitive to the value of colonial acquisitions for the purposes of trade. But, as a good radical, he was chiefly interested in putting into effect the principle of self-determination, and in trying to make the colonists run their own affairs for themselves.

* 31 March 1897. Speech by Chamberlain. Charles W. Boyd: *Mr. Chamberlain's Speeches,* II, 1-2.

APPENDIX II

A CRITICAL EXAMINATION OF THE BRITISH BLUE BOOKS AND GERMAN WHITE BOOK ON SOUTH WEST AFRICA

THE German White Book and the three British Blue Books on Angra Pequena do not tell the whole story of the dispute on this subject, voluminous though they are. This study has attempted to complete the story in the light of the material that has not been published. Many of the documents used in this book would in no case have been included in official publications. Private letters, documents containing confidential information, notes and despatches that were drafted but not sent, departmental minutes—the omission of all these from the Blue Books was a matter of course, although many of them are essential to a complete understanding of the negotiations.

But besides these, there were a number of important documents which were excluded from the official publications of the two governments concerned, and not infrequently documents that were published contained omissions or alterations of some importance. Since each government published such a full account of this incident, any study of the question that hopes to present fresh material must take as a starting point the omissions and alterations in the collections of documents that appeared at the time.

This course has been followed here, and while most of the omissions have already been described in the text or the notes, the subject is important enough to require a few additional remarks. This Appendix will discuss a little more fully several of the omissions that have been previously mentioned, in order to illustrate this method of approach, to show how the lacunae occurred and to indicate the most representative types of omission.

On 10 September 1883 Baron von Plessen called at the British foreign office and left a *Promemoria* inquiring whether England claimed suzerainty over Angra Pequena and, if so, on what ground the claim was based. This question was passed on to the colonial office in a letter of 22 September which was subsequently published in a British Blue Book with the omission of one paragraph, reading as follows: "I am to request that you will move the Earl of Derby to inform Lord Granville what answer should be returned to these inquiries."* This passage shows the lead thrown to the colonial office from the beginning; it is not, however, particularly important.

More significant is a deletion from the colonial office's reply, of 2 October 1883. This document began by stating that a British subject claimed to have prior rights of purchase over the territory stated to have been acquired by Lüderitz. It added that the islands adjacent to Angra Pequena had been annexed to the Cape Colony in 1867, "but that Her Majesty's Government have no claims or jurisdiction over the mainland." The words in quotation marks were omitted from the published version of this letter.† This passage was omitted because, five weeks later, the colonial office was induced by Mr. Scanlen, the premier of the Cape Colony, to change its mind. Scanlen urged the necessity of reserving the coast of South West Africa for British expansion, and, influenced by him, the colonial office wrote privately on 7 November 1883 asking the foreign office to postpone giving an answer to Germany,‡ and on 21 November wrote officially suggesting the terms of an answer to Count Münster.§ An answer in the words suggested by the colonial office was sent to Count Münster on the same day, stating that any claim to sovereignty in the territory in question would infringe legitimate British rights.|| The reason for the omission from the letter of the colonial office to the foreign office of 2 October is, therefore, that the answer to Count Münster suggested in the deleted passage was exactly the opposite of the answer which the colonial office suggested on 21 November 1883, and which was actually given.

* 22 September 1883. Foreign office to colonial office. British Blue Book, (C. 4190), No. 15. Full version in draft in F.O. 64/1101.

† 2 October 1883. Colonial office to foreign office. British Blue Book, (C. 4190), No. 16. Full version in F.O. 64/1101.

‡ 7 November 1883. Sir Robert G. W. Herbert to Sir Philip Currie. Private. F.O. 64/1101.

§ 21 November 1883. Colonial office to foreign office. F.O. 64/1101.

|| 21 November 1883. Lord Granville to Count Münster. British Blue Book, (C. 4190), No. 30.

The letter from the colonial office of 21 November 1883 was entirely omitted from the British Blue Book. Granville's note to Münster of the same date gave the same information and was written in almost the same words, and the colonial office letter was probably excluded, not only to avoid redundancy, but also because its publication would have emphasized, even more heavily than already appears in the Blue Book, the leadership of the colonial office.

On 14 June 1884 Granville wrote to Lord Ampthill giving an account of a conversation he had had with Count Herbert Bismarck on that day. When this despatch was afterwards published, two passages were deleted which contained statements attributed to Herbert Bismarck. In the first of these passages Count Bismarck admitted that the German views had not been quite so clearly stated as might have been done. In the second, he was reported to have said that Germany did not intend to establish "State Colonies" anywhere.* Another reference to "State Colonies," appearing in a letter to the colonial office, was also deleted.† Herbert Bismarck's damaging admission about the clarity of the German statements was clearly not the kind of remark that could be included in a Blue Book; it was a personal statement rather than an official one, and it was of a confidential character. The omission of the reference to "State Colonies" was made at the request of Prince Bismarck, and the term was deleted from the other document in which it appeared probably in order to conform to his wishes. On 3 July 1884 Lord Granville had communicated to the German embassy in London a copy of his despatch to Ampthill of 14 June. He explained that he intended to publish it in the forthcoming British Blue Book, and hoped that the German Government would not object to the inclusion in the despatch of Granville's statement that misunderstandings had occurred on both sides. The British Government was in a difficult parliamentary position, and Münster, noting that in this document England accepted the whole blame for the delay, sympathetically urged his government to assent to Granville's wishes (1).

Bismarck readily assented to the account of the conversation

* 14 June 1884. Lord Granville to Lord Ampthill. British Blue Book, (C. 4190), No. 69, Enclosure. Full version in F.O. 64/1102, despatch No. 169A. Draft. The passages referred to are given in Note 3 to Chapter V, p. 109.

† 12 July 1884. Foreign office to colonial office. British Blue Book, (C. 4190), No. 73. Full version in F.O. 64/1102.

given in Lord Granville's despatch, and questioned only the expression "State Colonies," which had been ascribed to Count Herbert Bismarck. The chancellor explained in a despatch to Münster of 12 July that this was a term difficult to define, and that in any case he could only give his opinion as to what was expedient for Germany at the present, and could not give an engagement for the future (2). He suggested a different wording, which was communicated to the British foreign office on 22 July 1884 by Baron von Plessen (3). This reading was adopted when the despatch was published in the Blue Book.

Granville's despatches to Ampthill of 18 and 21 June, describing his two later conversations with Count Herbert Bismarck, were omitted from the Blue Book entirely. This was done by arrangement with the German Government. Prince Bismarck had originally intended to publish Count Herbert Bismarck's despatches of 18 and 22 June 1884, dealing with the same conversations. Count Münster informed Lord Granville of this in December 1884, and added that since the British Government intended to publish Granville's despatch to Ampthill of 14 June describing his conversation with Herbert Bismarck, the German Government took it for granted "that there will be no objection to the publication of the two despatches which treat on the same subject." Granville replied that he could not tell whether he would object to the publication of Herbert Bismarck's despatches until he had seen them, and that since he had submitted to the German Government the papers which England intended to publish, he considered himself entitled to the same courtesy. He added that "we have not yet presented the papers, and I am quite ready to agree that the despatch of the 14th and indeed all record of these conversations should not appear."* Bismarck did not care for this suggestion, nor was he willing to admit the right of Lord Granville to see the German documents before they were published. He telegraphed to Münster on 7 December 1884: "I cannot understand how the idea can have occurred to Lord Granville, and, apparently, to your Excellency also, that the publication of his instructions of 14 June or of reports on his conversation with Count Bismarck could be undesired by us, so that he declares himself ready to omit them from the documents. On the contrary, this publication is necessary for us. . . ." Bis-

* 6 December 1884. Memorandum by Lord Granville. Secret and Confidential. F.O. 64/1105.

marck's telegram ended: "We agreed, in spite of this, out of courtesy, to Lord Granville's unexpected and purely formal request to have sent to him again the things that *he himself* intends to publish before *we* publish them; it is otherwise not usual that we, for the publication of the reports of *our own* officials, like Count Bismarck, obtain the consent of a foreign country" (4). On 8 December he telegraphed again to Münster that the degree of publicity intended by the British Government was sufficient for German needs, and that he would only publish the information contained in the documents that England intended to publish herself. While the publication of some report on Herbert Bismarck's conversations was necessary for Germany, it was best that the publications of the two governments should substantially correspond (5). Münster accordingly informed Lord Granville that Bismarck had no objection to the publication of Granville's despatch to Ampthill of 14 June, and that the German White Book "would contain nothing on the subject which could be objected to by Lord Granville, or be in disaccord with what His Lordship had reported."* The despatches describing Granville's conversations with Herbert Bismarck after 14 June were accordingly omitted by both governments from their respective publications, and when a question about this was asked later in Parliament, Lord Edmond Fitzmaurice, the under-secretary for foreign affairs, stated that: "It was agreed that the conversations between Lord Granville and Count Herbert Bismarck were of a confidential character."†

One other omission deserves to be mentioned. On 29 September 1884 Lord Granville wrote to the British chargé d'affaires in Berlin reporting a conversation with Baron von Plessen. England had just welcomed Germany as a neighbor on those parts of the southwest coast of Africa which were not actually in British possession, and Plessen now informed Granville that Prince Bismarck had observed that this was a step in the direction which he had hoped British policy would take, "and added that he could have wished in the interests of the present and the future that it had been taken earlier."‡ The omission of so critical a

* 13 December 1884. Foreign office to colonial office. Draft. F.O. 64/1105.

† 13 March 1885. *Hansard Parliamentary Debates,* CCXCV, 1077.

‡ 29 September 1884. Lord Granville to British chargé d'affaires in Berlin. British Blue Book, (C. 4262), No. 32, Enclosure. Full version in draft in F.O. 64/1103.

statement from so authoritative a source scarcely needs explanation.

These omissions are interesting, and some of them are fairly important, but, speaking generally, it cannot be said that the documents as they were presented in the Blue Books gave a false idea of that part of the negotiations which they covered. The lead in the negotiations which was taken by the colonial office is perfectly apparent from the Blue Books, although some of the passages which emphasize it most strongly were omitted. The passage in the letter from the colonial office of 2 October 1883 where it is suggested that Münster should be told that England had no claims on the mainland at Angra Pequena would certainly have been damaging if it had been included in a Blue Book, but, since this suggestion was canceled and never acted upon, the editors can hardly be criticized for leaving it out. There are, of course, many elements of British policy which do not appear in the Blue Books, such as the real opinions of the various cabinet members and permanent officials concerned, at different stages of the negotiations, the intentions they had which were not carried out, their personal inclinations and the influence of these upon their policy. To get this information we must go to private correspondence, to departmental minutes and to published memoirs and biographies. But as far as the acts of the British Government are concerned, the documents published give, on the whole, a roughly accurate account of the truth.

The German Government published only one White Book on Angra Pequena, a large collection of over sixty documents. This contained most of the important German documents of the kind that are usually included in a publication of this sort. (This excludes, of course, memoranda suggesting future policy, marginal comments, Bismarck's instructions to the foreign office, etc.) But the number of alterations made in the documents that were published was much greater than in the case of the British Blue Books. Not all these alterations were important: often a despatch or telegram was summarized for the sake of briefness or paraphrased for the sake of clarity. Certain changes, however, were significant.

On 4 February 1883 instructions were sent to Count Herbert Bismarck, the German chargé d'affaires in London, informing him of Lüderitz's plan to establish a trading station at Angra Pequena, and asking him to inquire if the British Government would be in a position to extend their protection to this undertaking. (These instructions are described on pages 28 ff.) In the passages left out of the White Book it was made clear that the protection which Germany would be prepared to give Lüderitz was only that protection which had customarily been given to German citizens residing abroad, and further, that Germany was now, as formerly, opposed to all oversea projects, and would only be pleased if England allowed her protection to extend to German settlers in those regions (6).

These instructions were executed by Count Herbert Bismarck on 7 February 1883, and their execution was reported by Münster on 26 February. Münster's despatch (described on page 31) explained that Sir Julian Pauncefote's attention had been especially called to the fact that Germany would be pleased if England were in the position to allow her protection to extend to the German settlements. But when Münster's despatch was published in the German White Book, this passage was left out (7).

The alterations in these two despatches were of great importance. It was Bismarck's contention, later, that he had dealt openly with the British Government, and had made perfectly clear his intention of placing Angra Pequena under German protection if it proved to be outside of British jurisdiction. The original wording of these despatches, however, shows that at the very beginning of the negotiations Bismarck had disclaimed a colonial policy. It was in the light of this statement, which was never contradicted, that the British Government interpreted Bismarck's later communications. This puts Bismarck's conduct in a less favorable light. The omission of these passages from the White Book indicates that the German authorities felt there was something to conceal.

On 18 August 1883 a despatch was sent to the German consul in Cape Town, informing him that Lüderitz's request for protection had been granted, and instructing him to help Lüderitz with advice and also to give him consular protection. In a passage omitted from the White Book, the consul was asked to recommend to Lüderitz especial reserve in the use of the press and to advise him not to discuss in the future the supposed attitude of the Imperial Government towards his projects (see pages 33-34) (8). Apart from the confidential nature of this passage, its extreme emphasis on reserve would not have looked altogether well in the White Book, where Bismarck tried to make out that he had proceeded openly with the British Government.

On 22 November 1883, Count Münster reported a conversation he had had with Lord Granville about Angra Pequena. In the course of this conversation, Lord Granville remarked "that he knew well that my government did not follow a colonial policy and also certainly did not intend to found a colony there." Granville's statement (which Münster seems to have accepted without opposition) was omitted from the White Book (9). The only thing in the German documents upon which Granville's statement could have been based was the despatch of 4 February 1883, which has already been discussed. The omissions from that document explain the omission of this passage too. Under ordinary circumstances it might well be a matter of indifference to the German Government what conception Granville had of their policy. But in this case, when Münster had, with some justification, executed his instructions in such a way as to give Granville the impression that Germany did not wish to pursue a colonial policy, it is comprehensible that the German Government should wish to cut out the passage in which it appeared how distinctly Granville had received this impression.

On 26 May 1884 Münster addressed to Bismarck a long despatch about Angra Pequena, reporting a number of conversations he had had with various people in London, and discussing the whole question in detail. In one passage of this despatch (described on pages 69-70) he made excuses for the attitude of the British Government and their delay, which he said was caused by the independence of the colonies and of the colonial secretary. This passage was omitted when the despatch was published in the White Book (10). All through the negotiations Bismarck protested that the reference by the British Government to the Cape Colony was nothing more than an evasion, and he repeatedly urged Münster not to accept this as an excuse for the delay that had occurred, and not to discuss the subject with Lord Derby, the colonial secretary. In this despatch Münster not only accepted the British explanation without protest, but he took the British side, and ventured to urge this explanation upon Bismarck. The despatch indicates that he was not executing his instructions properly, and had failed to represent Bismarck's views in the way that was desired. It would have been unusual to publish a passage in which the German ambassador took the British side of the argument.

Count Herbert Bismarck's two despatches of 17 and 22 June,

describing his two later conversations with Lord Granville, were omitted by arrangement with the British Government, as has already been related.

On 8 August 1884 Münster reported on a conversation with Lord Granville about the penal settlement condition. Granville said he was very sorry his latest communication had given offense, and that he had been under the impression that Count Herbert Bismarck had given his approval to the form in which it was drafted. This statement was omitted from Münster's despatch when it was published in the White Book, as was also a suggestion of Granville's that Lord Ampthill should ask for the return of the note in question, and that the communication should be redrafted in a form that the two governments should agree upon (11). Prince Bismarck strongly objected to the statement that the British communication had been concerted between Lord Granville and Count Herbert Bismarck, and Count Herbert Bismarck, when he was informed, denied that this was the case (see page 117). Bismarck considered that his son had not been empowered to discuss with the British Government the form of their next communication at all. Granville's suggestion that Lord Ampthill should withdraw his note was not agreed to by the German Government, and no reply was made to it. This would probably account for its omission from the White Book.

On 22 August 1884, instructions were sent to Baron von Plessen in London, requesting him to present a note to the British Government demanding that they should refuse to sanction the resolution of the Cape Parliament for the annexation of the coast of South West Africa. Besides this, the despatch to Plessen stated that if Granville brought up the subject of Lord Ampthill's note, he should reply that he had no instructions about that. For his personal information it was remarked that, since Lord Ampthill's note of 19 July 1884 had already been answered, the German Government attached no value to its withdrawal, and for that reason did not intend to give an answer to Lord Granville's proposal. The whole passage about Ampthill's note was omitted from this despatch when it was published in the White Book (12). The omission from this despatch was probably made for the same reason as the omission from Münster's report of 8 August. The passage in question concerned a suggestion made by the British Government which was not taken up, and the explanation added for Plessen's personal information was hardly the sort of thing to be included in an official publication.

The most serious alterations in the documents published in the German White Book were those made in the instructions of 4 February 1883 and the later despatches referring to it. The White Book gives the impression that Bismarck made his intentions fairly clear, while as a matter of fact he had, at the beginning of the negotiations, practically told the British Government in so many words that he had no intention of pursuing a colonial policy. Apart from this, the White Book gives a fairly truthful, though of course incomplete, account of the negotiations. That Münster did not execute his instructions very well is quite apparent from the White Book, although a number of passages were omitted in order to spare him. Bismarck's criticism of him on 1 June 1884, and Münster's long self-justification on 6 June, are of course documents of a confidential character and could not be included in a publication of this sort. We find no trace in the White Book of Bismarck's proposal, on 5 May 1884, for a general understanding with England on oversea matters, but this proposal covered a large field, and did not relate specifically to Angra Pequena.

NOTES

1. 3 July 1884. Count Münster to Prince Bismarck. No. 107. Reichsarchiv, Vermischtes Südwestafrika IV.

"Lord Granville theilte heute unter Rückerbittung den Entwurf eines vertraulichen Erlasses an Lord Ampthill bezüglich Angra Pequena's mit, von dem ich die gehorsamst beigefügte Abschrift genommen habe. Dieser Erlass wird im Blaubuch erscheinen: soviel ich zu beurtheilen vermag, dürften unserseits keine Einwendungen gegen den Inhalt zu erheben sein, da die englische Regierung die Schuld der Verzögerung in diesem Schriftstück rückhaltlos auf sich nimmt.

"Lord Granville bemerkte, die Stellung der Regierung dem Parlamente gegenüber in dieser Sache sei durch ihre eigene Schuld keine unanfechtbar (not quite clean); er würde deshalb dankbar sein, wenn wir ihm die Rückzugslinie 'es seien beiderseitige Missverständnisse vorgekommen' ohne Widerspruch offen liessen.

"Da die englische Regierung sachlich unseren Standpunkt vollkommen acceptirt, möchte ich empfehlen, ihr in dieser für uns irrelevanten façon de parler, auf die Lord Granville so grosses Gewicht legt, gefällig zu sein. . . ."

2. 12 July 1884. Instructions to Count Münster. Draft. Reichsarchiv, Vermischtes Südwestafrika IV.

The despatch states that Prince Bismarck has expressed agreement with Granville's account of the conversation of 14 June, "nur trage er Bedenken gegen die Fassung des mit 'In answer' beginnenden Absatzes. Denn der Begriff von 'State Colonies' lasse sich schwer definiren und konne Fürst Bismarck nur darüber, was *jetzt* für Deutschland zweckmässig sei, *seine*

Ansicht ausdrücken, seine Nachfolger und das Reich konne er aber nicht binden. . . .

"Vielleicht könnten die Worte nach 'he (Ct. Bismarck) stated that' bis zu they wished' gestrichen werden, sodass der Absatz etwa lauten würde: 'In answer to questions put by me, he stated that the German Government intended to give henceforth themselves full protection to Germans settling in (oder to German establishments in) uncivilized countries which were not under the sovereign jurisdiction of other European States.'"

3. 22 July 1884. Minute by Sir Julian Pauncefote on a conversation with Baron von Plessen. F.O. 64/1102.

"Baron Plessen asks with ref. to F.O. Despatch to Lord Ampthill No. 169A of 14 June 1884, (Marginal note: This is asked for the informon. of the Embassy here. J.P.) whether it still stands as the basis of arrangement? or whether it is superseded by a subsequent Despatch?

"Prince Bismarck would like a correction in Paragraph 4 (from the end) beginning, 'In answer' down to 'States.'

"Prince Bismarck would like the words, 'It was not the intention of the German Govt. to establish State Colonies anywhere but that' to be omitted. He does not quite understand precise meaning to be attached to the words 'State Colonies' and besides he cannot give any engagement *for the future*.

"He would be glad if the paragraph were altered thus.—'In answer to a question put by me, he stated that the German Govt. intended themselves to give henceforth full protection to Germans settling in (or to German Establishments in) uncivilized countries which were not under the Sovereign Jurisdiction of other European States.

"Count Münster will call on Lord Granville for a reply.

"J.P."

4. 7 December 1884. Prince Bismarck to Count Münster. Cipher telegram. No. 171. Reichsarchiv, Acta betr. Veröffentlichung I.

". . . Es ist mir nicht verständlich wie bei Lord Granville und, dem Anschein nach, auch bei Ew. p. der Gedanke hat enstehen können, dass uns die Veröffentlichung seines Erlasses vom 14. Juni oder von Andeutungen über seine Unterredung mit Graf Bismarck unerwünscht sein könne, so dass er sich bereit erklärt sie aus den Schriftstücken zu entfernen. Im Gegentheil liegt diese Veröffentlichung in unserem Bedürfniss und glaubte ich dass dieses auch für Ew. p. nicht zweifelhaft wäre. Mein Telegramm No. 169 ist nur die Folge von Ew. p. Telegramm No. 190 gewesen, nach welchem Lord Granville den *Anspruch* erhob, ebenso befragt zu werden wie er uns befragt hatte, obschon durch seine *Anfrage* schon die Zustimmung zu unserer *identischen* Veröffentlichung gegeben war. Wir sind ungeachtet dieser Thatsache auf Lord Granville's unerwarteten und rein formalen Anspruch, die Sachen, die *er selbst* veröffentlichen will von uns, bevor *wir* sie drucken, nochmals eingesandt zu erhalten, aus Höflichkeit eingegangen; es ist sonst nicht üblich, dass wir zum Abdruck der Berichte *unserer eigenen* Beamten, wie des Grafen Bismarck, fremde Zustimmung einholen. . . ."

5. 8 December 1884. Prince Bismarck to Count Münster. Cipher telegram. No. 172. Reichsarchiv, Acta betr. Veröffentlichung I.

". . . Für unsre Bedürfnisse genügt das Mass von Oeffentlichkeit, welches Lord Granville für die englische Veröffentlichung beabsichtigt hat. Weil ein Mehr ihm unerwünscht ist, deshalb wollen wir eben nur das aus Graf Bismarck's Berichten veröffentlichen, was in den Aktenstücken enthalten ist, die England selbst veröffentlichen zu wollen uns erklärt hat. In unserm Interesse liegt einerseits, dass diese Veröffentlichung *keinenfalls* unterbleibe, andererseits, dass die Veröffentlichungen beider Regierungen über denselben Vorgang im Wesentlichen übereinstimmen."

6. 4 February 1883. Instructions to Count Herbert Bismarck, German chargé d'affaires in London. German White Book, *Angra Pequena,* No. 2. Full version in draft in Reichsarchiv, Vermischtes Südwestafrika I. The text, with the omissions from the White Book, is given in Note 2 to Chapter II, p. 38.

7. 26 February 1883. Count Münster to Prince Bismarck. German White Book, *Angra Pequena,* No. 4. Full version in Reichsarchiv, Vermischtes Südwestafrika I. The passage omitted from the White Book has already been given, Chapter II, Note 3, p. 38.

8. 18 August 1883. Prince Bismarck to Lippert, the German consul in Cape Town. German White Book, *Angra Pequena,* No. 3. Full version in draft in Reichsarchiv, Vermischtes Südwestafrika I. The passage omitted from the White Book has been given in Chapter II, Note 6, p. 39.

9. 22 November 1883. Count Münster to Prince Bismarck. German White Book, *Angra Pequena,* No. 7. Full version in Reichsarchiv, Vermischtes Südwestafrika II. Part of the following paragraph was omitted from the White Book, the words omitted being indicated by italics:

"Lord Granville sagte mir, als er die Sache vorher mit mir besprach, *dass er ja wisse, dass meine hohe Regierung keine Colonial-Politik befolge und auch gewiss nicht beabsichtige, dort eine Colonie zu gründen.*"

10. 26 May 1884. Count Münster to Prince Bismarck. German White Book, *Angra Pequena,* No. 19. Full version in Reichsarchiv, Vermischtes Südwestafrika III. The passages omitted from the White Book have been given in Chapter IV, Note 10, pp. 85-86.

11. 8 August 1884. Count Münster to Prince Bismarck. German White Book, *Angra Pequena,* No. 37. Full version in Reichsarchiv, Vermischtes Südwestafrika V. The following passages do not appear in the White Book.

"Lord Granville begann unser Gespräch damit, dass er ausserordentlich bedauere, durch seine Note an Lord Ampthill Anstoss erregt zu haben. Er sei unter dem bestimmten Eindruck gewesen, dass die Note durch den Grafen Herbert Bismarck, mit dem er diese Angelegenheit vornehmlich verhandelt habe, gutgeheissen wurde. (Bismarck: das kann garnicht der Fall sein. Gr. H. B. ist garnicht in der Lage gewesen ein Wort über die Note zu äussern.)

". . . Soeben sah ich Lord Granville wieder und er sagte mir, dass er nach näherer Ueberlegung glaube, dass es am Besten sein würde, wenn Lord Ampthill seine Note zurückfordere und sie dann eine andere Fassung bekäme, die dann zu vereinbaren wäre. . . ."

12. 22 August 1884. Instructions to Baron von Plessen, the German chargé d'affaires in London. German White Book, *Angra Pequena,* No. 42. Full version in draft in Reichsarchiv, Vermischtes Südwestafrika VI. The following passages are omitted from the White Book.

"Solle Seine Excellenz Ihnen gegenüber die Note Lord Ampthill's vom 19. v. Mts. berühren, welche den Gegenstand des Berichts des Grafen Münster vom 8. d. Mts. bildet, so wollen Ew. pp. erwiedern, dass Ihnen hierüber noch keine Instruktion zugegangen sei.

"Zu Ihrer persönl. Information bemerke ich jedoch, dass der Herr Reichskanzler die Note als durch den Erlass vom 24. v. Mts. bereits beantwortet ansieht; die Zurückziehung derselben würde für uns keinen Werth haben; wir beabsichtigen deshalb nicht auf das Erbieten hierzu eine Antwort zu ertheilen. . . ."

APPENDIX III

COUNT HERBERT BISMARCK

HERBERT Count von Bismarck-Schönhausen, usually known as Count Herbert Bismarck, played so large a part in the Angra Pequena negotiations that it seems worth while, for the reader's information, to gather together a few of the principal facts about him. He was the eldest son of the great chancellor, and served under his father in many important capacities until both resigned from the government in 1890. He was born in 1849, served in the Franco-Prussian war, married Countess Margarete Hoyos in 1892, inherited the title of Prince upon his father's death in 1898, and died in 1904.

However limited may have been Count Herbert Bismarck's abilities, there can be no question that he performed great and useful services for his father, work which he alone, because of his personal position, was able to do. In the years 1882-86 he served as an unofficial connecting link between Prince Bismarck and members of the English political world and occasionally carried out special missions. In the years 1886-90, when he was foreign secretary, he acted again as a connecting link, this time between his father and the German foreign office. The work done by Herbert Bismarck was not dramatic, nor did it require great originality or talent, but it was a work that he alone was competent to perform, and it was of the greatest value to Prince Bismarck.

Herbert Bismarck entered the foreign service in 1874, at the age of twenty-five, and served until 1881, with occasional interruptions, as his father's private secretary. After 1881 Prince Bismarck sent him to the important diplomatic centers of Europe in turn, London, Paris, St. Petersburg, The Hague, and Vienna. In these visits, Herbert was sometimes attached in an official capacity to an embassy and sometimes sent on special missions. After Count Hatzfeldt, the foreign secretary, had been made ambassador to London in 1885, Herbert acted in his position at the foreign office, and in May 1886 became secretary of state himself. This position he retained until he left office in March 1890. Besides all this, he was for some years an active member of the Reichstag.*

In 1881, just before his visit to England, Herbert Bismarck had an unfortunate love affair with the Princess Elizabeth Carolath, who was the daughter of Prince Hatzfeldt-Trachenberg and the sister-in-law of Field Marshal Baron Walter von Loë. The Princess had procured a divorce from her husband, Prince Carolath-Beuthen, with the intention of marrying Herbert Bismarck. Not only was Princess Carolath a divorcée, not only was she a member of the eccentric Hatzfeldt family, but she was related by marriage to the families of Loë and Schleinitz, which included some of Prince Bismarck's bitterest political enemies. Prince Bismarck set himself violently against the match and told Herbert it was incompatible with his sense of honor that his name should be allied by marriage with the names of Princess Carolath and her relatives. In April 1881 Herbert wrote to his friend Eulenburg that his father, in tears, had informed him that it was his fixed decision to live no longer if the marriage took place. The altercation was carried on with the utmost passion on both sides. When Herbert wished to visit Princess Carolath in Venice, the chancellor threatened to travel to Venice with him, international complications notwithstanding, and declared that the prevention of this marriage was of greater importance to him than the empire, his work, and what remained to him of his life.†

Prince Bismarck had his way and the match was broken off, but the incident had a deep effect on Herbert, who was bitterly disappointed and could not rid himself of the feeling that he had not treated the Princess fairly.‡

Whether this tragedy embittered Herbert and made him harsher in all his personal relationships, it is impossible to say. Eulenburg asserts that he possessed an extraordinary charm before this experience came to him.§ In any case it is certain that in conversation and personal contact with friends Herbert was frequently rough and overbearing. On the other hand, descriptions

* Wolfgang Windelband: *Herbert Bismarck als Mitarbeiter seines Vaters,* pp. 6-7.

† Fürst Eulenburg: *Aus 50 Jahren,* pp. 81, 86, 87, 92, 93, 95.

‡ *Ibid.,* p. 101. Prince Bülow: *Memoirs,* IV, 261, 586.

§ Fürst Eulenburg: *Aus 50 Jahren,* p. 81.

of him often contradict each other, so that it is not clear whether his manner was merely rough and careless or wholly intolerable.

In England, especially on his earlier visits, he was generally well liked. Granville received him most warmly, as related at the beginning of Chapter I, and wrote to Ampthill that it "was impossible for anyone to be more genial and easily pleased."* Dilke took a liking to him when he first came to England, and later referred to him as "this personally friendly fellow."† When, in January 1884, Herbert Bismarck left London for St. Petersburg, Lord Granville wrote to him: "It is not usual to express one's regrets in writing to a Secretary of Embassy on his change of post. But the case is different of one who partly from his personal position but still more from his abilities and personal qualities has done so much to strengthen the good relations of the two Countries. . . . I was truly sorry to hear of your leaving us. . . . You know the welcome you will receive from all, if you return."‡

But in June 1884 Herbert Bismarck returned to England under less pleasant conditions. He came to put the German case in regard to Angra Pequena, and, since the real reason for his being sent was that Münster would not stand up for German interests, Herbert's protests were energetic and aroused some British resentment. Dilke, as mentioned on page 94, says he was very rude to Lord Granville, and Busch reports that Prince Bismarck showed a letter to Bucher, his private secretary, in which it was described how Herbert had replied to an inquiry of Granville's that it was "a question of mere curiosity," and indeed finally, "a matter that does not concern you."§ (This letter is undoubtedly the despatch of 17 June 1884, described on page 96.)

Maximilian von Hagen, in his book on Bismarck's colonial policy, explains Dilke's assertion on the ground that any firm statement of German colonial views was at that time so completely unexpected by the English that it might well have given the impression of rudeness that Dilke describes. Busch's accusations, Hagen points out, were based on third-hand information and savor of jealousy, since Herbert was disliked by the sub-

* 21 December 1881. Lord Granville to Lord Ampthill. Lord Edmond Fitzmaurice: *Life of Lord Granville,* II, 256.

† Gwynn and Tuckwell: *Life of Sir Charles W. Dilke,* I, 432; II, 99-100.

‡ 15 January 1884. Lord Granville to Count Herbert Bismarck. Draft. Private. Private Granville MSS, G.D. 29/207.

§ M. Busch: *Bismarck, Some Secret Pages of His History,* III, 120.

ordinates of Bismarck, especially by Bucher, through whom this information came.* There is something in Hagen's arguments, and it is certainly true that Herbert Bismarck continued on pleasant terms with Granville and other British statesmen after 1884, though Dilke thought, seriously perhaps, that young Bismarck was trying to secure the dismissal of Granville and Derby in March 1885, an exaggeration that illustrates the British feeling at the time.† We know in any case that Bucher did not exaggerate Herbert Bismarck's report of his interview with Granville (see page 96). There are, moreover, too many references to the overbearing manners, rudeness, and tactlessness of Herbert Bismarck for us to believe that his conduct in general was so correct and courteous as Hagen makes out.

Bismarck himself once said to Busch:‡ "You seem not to have been able to get on with my son Herbert, the new Secretary of State? Yes, yes, my son is not yet forty, and more obstinate and self-assertive than I am even to-day, after successes which not even my enemies belittle." (It was, as a matter of fact, Privy-Councillor Holstein and not Herbert Bismarck with whom Busch had had difficulty.) Even Prince Bülow, who had a genuine liking for Herbert, bore witness to his want of tact: "The Secretary of State, Herbert Bismarck, who accompanied the Kaiser in 1888 [to Italy], only intensified his Sovereign's faults and mistakes by his own behavior. Although he was rich in qualities of the heart and of the head, he was often deficient in tact. This was particularly noticeable on the very difficult Roman terrain."§ The Countess Kleinmichel told Prince Hohenlohe in 1888 that Herbert Bismarck, when secretary of embassy at St. Petersburg, was "brutal," and sought to make a parade of it. On his arrival he had said to the gentlemen of the staff that they must not be too polite to the Russians.|| Bülow tells another story, that, when he was at the foreign office in 1897, "a commissionaire entered, or rather came jumping in, and requested me to see the Foreign Secretary. Herbert Bismarck had trained the messengers to act in this way. He had kept them in such a permanent state of

* Maximilian von Hagen: *Bismarcks Kolonialpolitik,* pp. 170, 365.

† Gwynn and Tuckwell: *Life of Sir Charles W. Dilke,* II, 99.

‡ This was Dr. Klemens Busch, the under-secretary of state in the foreign office, not Moritz Busch, elsewhere referred to, who assisted Bismarck in relations with the press.

§ Prince Bülow: *Memoirs,* IV, 348, 623.

|| Prince Hohenlohe: *Memoirs,* II, 408.

tension and fear that when he rang his bell they would dash into his room like a trout when it leaps over an obstruction."*

In March 1886 Count Waldersee (the later chief of the general staff) criticized Herbert Bismarck's whole attitude. He said Herbert had become accustomed to act as if he were his father; "but unfortunately he lacks the understanding of the father, and also his fine sense of tact." If Herbert, argued Waldersee, "would act tactfully in his present position, and use his influence to soothe instead of to annoy, as he does now, he would have a great future before him; by his present conduct he must ruin himself completely."†

In June 1888 the Empress Frederick told Prince Hohenlohe that "Herbert Bismarck had had the effrontery to say to the Prince of Wales that an Emperor who couldn't talk was not fit to reign. The Prince had said that had he not valued the good relations between England and Germany he would have thrown him out of the room." This anecdote may have taken on color in passing through the hands of the Empress Frederick, whose relations to the Bismarck family were never very friendly. But on the same day Prince Hohenlohe found the Prince of Wales himself "exceedingly angered at the boorishness of the Bismarck family, father and son."‡ And Lord Rosebery, who shortly afterwards at Sandringham heard a long narrative from the Prince of Wales of what had passed during his visit to Berlin, found him still "very indignant."§

These accounts of Herbert Bismarck contrast strangely with, for example, the description Gladstone gave of him in March 1885: "He spoke in a modest and thoroughly friendly manner. . . . I cannot presume to answer for any practical result, but nothing could be more rational or more friendly than the conversation."‖ But there is no real difficulty in reconciling these contradictory descriptions of Herbert's bearing. The phenomenon of a man who is rude at times and at other times agreeable is by no means uncommon. It is unlikely that Herbert Bismarck, in the course of his education, should have failed to become familiar with the

* Prince Bülow: *Memoirs,* I, 7-8.

† *Denkwürdigkeiten des General-Feldmarschalls Alfred Grafen von Waldersee,* I, 275-76.

‡ Prince Hohenlohe: *Memoirs,* II, 402-03.

§ Marquess of Crewe: *Lord Rosebery,* I, 328.

‖ 5-6 March 1885. Mr. Gladstone to Lord Granville. Lord Edmond Fitzmaurice: *Life of Lord Granville,* II, 430-31.

ordinary decencies of social intercourse. His father, as is well known, could display upon occasion the greatest cordiality and charm. But if Herbert inherited some social talent from his father, he also unquestionably inherited his arrogant and overbearing qualities, which in Herbert, with his lesser gifts, must have been almost unendurable. Even those who knew him well and were deeply attached to him, like Bülow or Lord Rosebery, fully admit the bluntness of his manners.*

Herbert Bismarck was no genius, but he was not without abilities of a certain order. He was clever and industrious, as even Waldersee admitted in 1886, though he was no friend to Herbert at that time.† What ability he had was developed to the utmost by his extraordinary training. Bucher allowed that he had a good memory, and mentioned that Herbert had been "a great deal with his father. He was often present at interviews with important personages, at which matters of great moment were discussed that do not appear in the official documents, and in that way he has had splendid opportunities for learning." Bucher never liked Herbert, but his opinion of Herbert's ability rose in the course of time. Thus in November 1881 he said: "He [Hatzfeldt] will be replaced by Herbert, that haughty and incapable fellow, and more than one of the officials will leave." But Herbert's success in the London negotiations of June 1884 made a more favorable impression on the private secretary. On 23 September 1884 Bucher admitted to Busch that Herbert was "very diligent and not unskilful," and said, regarding Herbert's becoming head of the foreign office: "It will not be pleasant to work under the young man, but work will be done, and things will not be allowed to drag on in such a slow and slovenly way."‡

One important service performed by Herbert Bismarck in his visits to England was the collection of information. In July 1882 Busch noted that Herbert was sending his father, Holstein, or Rantzau "private reports of what he picked up in London society, the clubs, etc.—mostly gossip—which was then forwarded to the Emperor and occasionally made use of in the press." He sent this information directly, instead of communicating it to Münster and

* Prince Bülow: *Memoirs,* IV, 348. Marquess of Crewe: *Lord Rosebery,* II, 549-50.

† *Denkwürdigkeiten des General-Feldmarschalls Alfred Grafen von Waldersee,* I, 282.

‡ M. Busch: *Bismarck, Some Secret Pages of His History,* III, 15, 118-19.

letting him forward it, which would have been the correct procedure.* Herbert's exceptional position in London society, added to his personal position in Berlin, enabled him not only to pick up gossip but to ascertain the opinions of leading English statesmen who might or might not be in agreement with the British official policy. He was able to talk over matters with a freedom and informality which were impossible for Münster, in his official position, and the closeness of his connection with the German chancellor secured him a hearing under all circumstances. In 1884 Herbert Bismarck discussed the policy of Granville and Derby with other members of the cabinet with extraordinary frankness, and was able to send his father sharp criticisms of the policy of the British Government, made by men who were actually members of that government.

In 1884 and 1885 Herbert Bismarck went on two special missions to London in connection with the German colonial question. The mission of June-July 1884 has already been fully described in Chapter V. A word may be said here about the second mission, in March 1885, which comes outside the scope of this book. Its purpose was to arrange a settlement of the disputed territorial claims of Germany and England in different parts of the world. The negotiations resulted in a compromise, England making concessions in New Guinea and Germany making concessions in Bechuanaland and St. Lucia Bay. Bucher severly criticized the arrangement Herbert Bismarck had made: "He [Herbert] does not understand, for instance, that colonies require a coast if they are to prosper, and so he made concessions which we are now trying to alter. He allows himself to be won over too easily. Rosebery has been particularly successful in that, and has quite mesmerized him." At another time Bucher said: "Herbert, who was not sufficiently well acquainted with the maps, etc., conceded too much to Rosebery, who was very sharp, so that the result was disadvantageous to us."† This is not the place to enter on a discussion of these negotiations and the advantages to Germany that they secured, a debatable subject in any case. For present purposes it may be pointed out that Bucher's view is not universal, either among contemporary observers or among scholars. Waldersee wrote at the time that "Herbert Bismarck has achieved

* M. Busch: *Bismarck, Some Secret Pages of His History,* III, 60.

† *Ibid.,* III, 135–36, 144.

a decided success."* Hagen declares that Prince Bismarck was acting from the point of view of general policy and wanted to placate England by moderation.† Rothfels insists that the German concessions in South Africa merely corresponded to the English concessions in New Guinea.‡

When Herbert Bismarck assumed charge of the German foreign office at the end of 1885, the character of his work changed. In these last years, when Prince Bismarck saw less and less of foreign diplomats and ministers, it was left largely up to Herbert to conduct personal negotiations. To Herbert also fell the responsibility for managing the foreign office, and he acted as the medium of communication between Bismarck and the German ministers. To some extent he also handled his father's communications with the emperor, the crown prince, and Prince Wilhelm.§ These duties were very heavy, and if Herbert had not been available to perform them, and to perform them effectively, they must have fallen on his father. Except for the Prince's younger son, Count Wilhelm Bismarck (who was indeed also pressed into service), no one else could possibly have undertaken this work. For the chancellor, who was old and in poor health, the advantage of this assistance was tremendous.

Prince Hohenlohe recorded on 26 May 1888: "Bleichröder maintains that Bismarck leaves his son too free a hand."|| Waldersee also, in March 1886, thought Bismarck wonderfully under his son's influence, and said later that Herbert deviated from his father's policy in small nuances.¶ Bülow asserts that Herbert influenced his father on the question of Bülow's promotion.** It is not to be inferred, however, that Herbert exercised any control over major questions of policy. It was natural that he should try to intervene in the matter of the promotion of an intimate friend, but, even if Bülow's story is true, the issue was relatively unimportant. The fact that Herbert, during his last

* *Denkwürdigkeiten des General-Feldmarschalls Alfred Grafen von Waldersee*, I, 253.

† Maximilian von Hagen: *Bismarcks Kolonialpolitik*, pp. 485-86.

‡ Hans Rothfels: *Bismarcks Englische Bündnispolitik*, p. 88.

§ Wolfgang Windelband: *Herbert Bismarck als Mitarbeiter seines Vaters*, pp. 20-21.

|| Prince Hohenlohe: *Memoirs*, II, 400.

¶ *Denkwürdigkeiten des General-Feldmarschalls Alfred Grafen von Waldersee*, I, 279, 363.

** Prince Bülow: *Memoirs*, IV, 617.

five years of office, was in a position of the greatest responsibility meant that the decision on innumerable details was left to him. Also, there is no doubt that both then and earlier Bismarck relied on Herbert's reports of confidential interviews as a basis for many of his diplomatic actions, and to this extent Herbert did exert an influence on his father. But the policy pursued was always Bismarck's own; Herbert may have initiated plans of immediate action but there is nothing to show that he took any share in determining the ends that German policy was designed to achieve.

The part that Herbert Bismarck played in the affairs of his father was thus a minor one. He differs from other statesmen in that he was never carrying out a policy of his own. What he could do, and did with enormous success, was to act as an instrument of his father, almost as an extension of his father's personality. This brings the character of his services almost down to the level of those of a private secretary, but he did work which no one else could have done and which was of the greatest importance to Bismarck.

APPENDIX IV

GLADSTONE'S POSITION ON THE GERMAN COLONIAL QUESTION*

GLADSTONE did not take an active part in the German colonial negotiations until the question of South West Africa was on a fair way to settlement. In the negotiations on the later German colonies, however, notably New Guinea, his influence made itself felt. When he did intervene his attitude was, in contrast to that of his colleagues, consistent and decided. He was quite clear in his own mind that England had no need of further colonies, he had no objection to German colonization and, while he was not intimidated by Bismarck, he saw no reason to give offense to Germany by seizing lands which she wanted and England did not.

In regard to Angra Pequena Gladstone was apparently not consulted until the negotiations had reached a climax. This is the more surprising because he took an active interest in foreign affairs, especially at periods of crisis. During the Franco-Prussian War he is said to have held "almost daily conferences with Lord Granville at the foreign office,"† which by the way is probably one of the reasons why Granville was more successful as a foreign minister in 1870 than in 1884. In the case of the German colonies, however, the first reference to the subject in Gladstone's private correspondence is in a letter of 1 August 1884, which is about New Guinea, and Angra Pequena is first mentioned (and briefly at that) in a letter to Granville of 5 September,‡ whereas, after September 1884, Gladstone is discussing German colonies continually. Nor is there any evidence in the official documents of

* For a fuller discussion of Gladstone's attitude on foreign affairs in this period the reader is referred to Paul Knaplund: *Gladstone's Foreign Policy.* (New York, 1935.) Mr. Knaplund has used the Gladstone Papers and quotes from several of the documents mentioned in this Appendix.

† John Morley: *Life of Gladstone,* II, 338.

‡ 1 August 1884. Mr. Gladstone to Lord Derby. Copy. Private Gladstone MSS, Gladstone Letter Book, Vol. 21, p. 180. 5 September 1884. Mr. Gladstone to Lord Granville. Copy. *Ibid.,* Vol. 21, p. 209.

the foreign office that Gladstone was consulted before 14 June 1884, when the matter was discussed in cabinet. The reason for this is probably that Granville himself did not realize until June, when Herbert Bismarck took over the negotiations, that Germany wanted to lay claim to Angra Pequena. All this only goes to show how completely Granville misunderstood Bismarck's intentions.

Gladstone, of course, had no liking for colonial annexations. His belief in free trade removed one of the principal reasons for colonies, and his theory of imperial defense, that is defense of the colonies by themselves and extrication of the British occupying armies, made him averse to fresh annexations which would mean more use of English armies abroad.* It followed logically that England could have no objection to German colonization. Gladstone wrote to Granville in December 1884: "I would give Bismarck every satisfaction about his Colonial matters, and I am ashamed at the panic about Germany in South Africa."† Of Bismarck's colonial acquisitions he wrote: "But as to the things done, in themselves, I do not know whether we have reason to complain?" Regarding proposed further British expansion he added: "I see great objection to it; and generally, considering what we have got I am against entering into a scramble for the remainder."‡ To Derby he wrote: "Is it dignified, or is it required by any real interest, to make extensions of British authority without any view of occupying but simply to keep them [the Germans] out? Is it not open to a strong positive objection in regard to the coast now in question between St. Lucia Bay and Delagoa Bay? Namely that it tends powerfully to entail a responsibility for the country lying inland, which we think it impolitic to assume? And which in the case of Zululand we have publicly and expressly renounced?"§

Gladstone even went so far as to welcome German colonization on the ground that it strengthened England's hold upon the colonies she already possessed. Writing to Derby on 21 December 1884 he declared: "And for my part I should be extremely glad to see the Germans become our neighbors in South Africa, or even

* For a fuller discussion of Gladstone's views on imperial expansion see Chapter I, pp. 5 ff.

† 7 December 1884. Mr. Gladstone to Lord Granville. Private Granville MSS, G.D. 29/128.

‡ 28 December 1884. Mr. Gladstone to Lord Granville No. 1. Private Granville MSS, G.D. 29/128.

§ 30 December 1884. Mr. Gladstone to Lord Derby. Draft. Private Gladstone MSS.

the neighbors of the Transvaal. We have to remember Chatham's conquest of Canada, so infinitely lauded, which killed dead as mutton our best security for keeping the British Provinces."* In January 1885 he wrote to Granville: "I see my way clearly to this that German colonization will strengthen and not weaken our hold upon our Colonies: and will make it very difficult for them to maintain the domineering tone to which their public organs are too much inclined."† These opinions are strikingly far-sighted.

Feeling as he did about new annexations, Gladstone was not likely to let himself be stampeded by the expansionist demands of the colonies. But he recognized that England must consult with them, and thought this should be explained to Bismarck. The point was "that there are three parties in the field, not two; that we have to act in the face of great colonial communities which will have, and which know that they will have, preponderating power in the Southern Levant (so to call it), and which mean not only to argue but to bully in this matter. For this point in the situation Foreign States ought to make some allowance." However, while he acknowledged the importance of the colonial communities, he refused to let them dictate to him. The letter to Granville continues: "I for my part, and I think you, do not mean to be bullied by them, but I am not sure that all our colleagues are altogether like-minded."‡

Although he had no objection to the German colonial program, Gladstone was slow to realize the connection between the colonial controversy and Bismarck's unfriendly policy in Egypt. He wrote to Granville in September 1884: "On reading H. Bismarck's letter . . . I incline to suppose it admits that his father's conduct in the [Egyptian] conference was a return slap for Angra Pequena."§ This is an extraordinary statement, in view of the fact that Bismarck had for months been trying to make the British Government understand that he would support them in Egypt only in exchange for colonial favors, and it shows how far Gladstone was out of touch with the negotiations at that stage. But later, when he understood Bismarck's position and saw that a

* 21 December 1884. Mr. Gladstone to Lord Derby. Copy. Private. Private Gladstone MSS, Gladstone Letter Book, Vol. 21, p. 301.

† 29 January 1885. Mr. Gladstone to Lord Granville. Private. Private Granville MSS, G.D. 29/129.

‡ 29 January 1885. Mr. Gladstone to Lord Granville. Private. Private Granville MSS, G.D. 29/129.

§ 5 September 1884. Mr. Gladstone to Lord Granville. *Ibid.*, G.D. 29/128.

bargain was being proposed, he hastened to show his readiness to trade, and made every effort to dispose of the colonial question as expeditiously as possible in order to clear the way for Britain's main concern, which was Egypt. With Derby he remonstrated: "No doubt we must be most cautious here as to colonial alarmism; but any language at Berlin appearing to convey sympathy with it might at this moment do extraordinary mischief to us at our one really vulnerable point, Egypt."* On 6 March 1885, after a long conversation the day before with Herbert Bismarck, in which the latter explained the German policy, Gladstone wrote to Granville: "Now I do hope that you are pressing forward the Pauncefote settlement for the North Coast of New Guinea which seems to me the main or only point remaining. It is really impossible to exaggerate the importance of getting out of the way the bar to the Egyptian settlement. These words strong as they are are in my opinion words of truth and soberness as, if we cannot wind up at once these small colonial controversies we shall, before we are many weeks older, find to our cost."†

This far Gladstone was willing to coöperate with Bismarck. He did not care about annexations, and he was ready to let Bismarck please himself so long as no obstacle was placed in the way of England's handling of the Egyptian situation. But this did not mean that he was subservient to Bismarck or could be bullied by the chancellor's threats about Egypt. The evidence is all the other way. In September 1884 Granville wrote to say that a rumor had reached him through several sources that "Bismarck is very angry, that he will defend the rights of the German Indemnity and bond holders that he will oppose illegal action on the part of the Egyptians, and gives as an ultimate [sic] ratio, the mandate of Europe to France, and in his opinion we should not like to face this. A despatch also came in yesterday from Paget, which you have probably not yet seen, giving Kalnoky's opinion that we must no longer reckon upon Bismarck's friendly support in Egypt."‡ Gladstone replied: "Bismarck's fuming does not much alarm me. Turkey and Italy would be fair allies against a man-

* 24 December 1884. Mr. Gladstone to Lord Derby. Copy. Private Gladstone MSS, Gladstone Letter Book, Vol. 21, p. 305.

† 6 March 1885. Mr. Gladstone to Lord Granville. Copy. Private Gladstone MSS, Gladstone Letter Book, Vol. 21, p. 366.

‡ 1 September 1884. Lord Granville to Mr. Gladstone. Private Gladstone MSS.

date to France; nor am I sure that Russia would join in it."* Later Gladstone wrote, regarding another proposal of Bismarck's: "If by improved finance and more cheerful calculations the Coupon can be saved, well and good. . . . But as to using British credit proper to make the Bondholders Dividend, I much doubt whether the Cabinet will ask it, I do not believe Parliament will grant it unless it be as part of a Jingo policy, and I do not quite see what it is that Bismarck and his obedient Powers are to do against the Government of Egypt backed and approved by us."†

Enough has been said to show how marked was the difference between Gladstone's attitude on the later German colonies and that of his colleagues on South West Africa. He was willing to purchase assistance in Egypt from Bismarck by colonial concessions, but he was convinced that Bismarck was nothing to be afraid of, and that on matters concerning Egypt England need not give in to German pressure. But he was in favor of treating Germany well in colonial matters, not only for reasons of expediency but also because he felt England had no legitimate objection to German colonization and that the right in several points of controversy was on Germany's side.

This is an aspect of Gladstone's policy that has not been sufficiently emphasized. The key to many of his political actions can be found in the religious side of his character. This is true of so few statesmen in modern times that we are apt to forget it was so in Gladstone's case. A passionately devout man, it was his object to incorporate the teachings of religion into his conduct of public affairs, and he did this at times with a disconcerting literalness. He employed not only his own talents but also the powers of the state for religious or moral purposes, and an ethical current runs through many fields of his activity. In foreign affairs, not his principal interest, the two occasions on which he took a most conspicuous part were the freeing of Italy and the rescuing of the Christian populations in the Balkans from Turkish government. Similarly, in the German colonial question he was constantly appealing to principles of equity. "I suppose," he wrote, "Bismarck ought to learn from us that whatever be his under-

* 2 September 1884. Mr. Gladstone to Lord Granville. Private Granville MSS, G.D. 29/128.

† 17 October 1884. Mr. Gladstone to Lord Granville. Copy. Private Gladstone MSS, Gladstone Letter Book, Vol. 21, pp. 249-50.

standings elsewhere and his present intentions towards us, we shall endeavor in every question to be guided by permanent and not fugitive considerations and to treat every German claim which may concern us in an equitable spirit."* He was always ready to look at things from the German point of view: "He [Bulwer] says it would be an act of palpable unfriendliness for the Germans to set themselves down *by us.* This is the very thing we (wisely and properly) did on the North Coast of New Guinea!"†

In fact the reason which Gladstone most frequently urged for concessions to Bismarck was the justice of Bismarck's cause. Writing to Granville about Bismarck and Angra Pequena, he said: "But he seems to have had such a case that I no longer grudge your consulting Germany about New Guinea."‡ A few months later he wrote again to Granville that coöperation with Germany was of "immense importance" and that he himself was ready for it "because I think that as far as I understand the matters at issue the Germans are on the most of them substantially right."§

* 29 January 1885. Mr. Gladstone to Lord Granville. Private. Private Granville MSS, G.D. 29/129.

† 31 March 1885. Mr. Gladstone to Lord Derby. Copy. Private Gladstone MSS, Gladstone Letter Book, Vol. 21, p. 384.

‡ 5 September 1884. Mr. Gladstone to Lord Granville. Copy. Private Gladstone MSS, Gladstone Letter Book, Vol. 21, p. 209.

§ 31 December 1884. Mr. Gladstone to Lord Granville. Private Granville MSS, G.D. 29/129.

BIBLIOGRAPHY

(This Bibliography makes no attempt to be complete; it merely lists the full titles of the sources quoted or referred to in this book, together with a few additional works of which special use has been made.)

UNPUBLISHED DOCUMENTARY SOURCES

Official Records

F.O.—Foreign Office Papers. Public Record Office, London.

Reichsarchiv, Vermischtes Südwestafrika.—Auswärtiges Amt. Kolonial-Abtheilung. A II. Acta secreta betr. die Handelsfactorei des Kaufmanns F.A.E. Lüderitz in Angra Pequena. (Süd-West Africa). Vermischtes Südwestafrika. Reichsarchiv, Berlin.

Reichsarchiv, Vermischtes Neu-Guinea.—Auswärtiges Amt. Kolonial-Abtheilung. A III. Acta betr. die diesseitigen Beziehungen zu den Marschall Inseln, Carolinen, Duke of York Inseln, Neu-Irland und Neu-Britannien, sowie den Ralick- und Ellive-Inseln pp. Vermischtes Neu-Guinea. Reichsarchiv, Berlin.

Reichsarchiv, Acta betr. Veröffentlichung.—Auswärtiges Amt. Kolonial-Abtheilung. A II. Acta betr. Veröffentlichung der Angra Pequena betreffenden diplomatischen Aktenstücke. Reichsarchiv, Berlin.

Private Papers

Private Granville MSS, G.D.—Papers of the second Earl Granville. Gifts and Deposits, Public Record Office, London.

Private Gladstone MSS.—Papers of William Ewart Gladstone. British Museum, London.

PUBLISHED DOCUMENTARY SOURCES

British Blue Books

The British Blue Books on South West Africa and New Guinea are in the following volumes of *Accounts and Papers:*

1881, Vol. LXVI

(C. 2754). *Copy of a Despatch from the Right Hon. the Earl of Kimberley, containing the instructions addressed to Governor Sir H. Robinson, G.C.M.G., on his departure to assume the offices of Governor of the Cape and High Commissioner in South Africa.* Presented January 1881.

1884, Vol. LVI

(C. 4190). *Correspondence respecting the settlement at Angra Pequena, on the S.W. Coast of Africa.* Presented August 1884.

1884-5, Vol. LIV

(C. 4217). *Further Correspondence respecting New Guinea and Other Islands, and the Convention at Sydney of Representatives of the Australian Colonies.* Presented October 1884.

(C. 4273). *Further Correspondence respecting New Guinea and Other Islands in the Western Pacific Ocean.* Presented February 1885.

(C. 4441). *Arrangement between Great Britain and Germany relative to their respective Spheres of Action in Portions of New Guinea.* Presented June 1885.

1884-5, Vol. LV

(C. 4442). *Arrangement between Great Britain and Germany relative to their respective Spheres of Action in Portions of Africa.* Presented June 1885.

1884-5, Vol. LVI

(C. 4262). *Further Correspondence respecting the Settlement at Angra Pequena on the South-West Coast of Africa.* Presented December 1884.

(C. 4265). *Copy of a Despatch from the Right Honourable the Earl of Derby, K.G., to Her Majesty's High Commissioner in South Africa, relative to the Establishment of a German Protectorate at Angra Pequena and along the neighboring Coast.* Presented December 1884.

German White Books

The German White Books relating to colonial matters are to be found in the *Stenographische Berichte über die Verhandlungen des Reichstages.* 6. Legislaturperiode.—I. Session 1884/85. Volumes V, VI, and VII. The important ones are as follows:

Togogebiet und Biafra-Bai. Presented 4 December 1884. Vol. V, pp. 114-43.

Angra Pequena. Presented 11 December 1884. Vol. V, pp. 159-87.

Deutsche Interessen in der Südsee. Presented 12 December 1884. Vol. V, pp. 197-231.

Deutsche Land-Reklamationen auf Fidji. Presented 19 January 1885. Vol. V, pp. 419-55.

Deutsche Interessen in der Südsee. II. Presented 5 February 1885. Vol. VI, pp. 687-728.

Aktenstücke betreffend die Kongo-Frage. Presented 8 April 1885. Vol. VII, pp. 1641-70.

Aktenstücke betreffend Ägypten. Presented 5 May 1885. Vol. VII, pp. 1879-97.

Other published documentary sources

Die Grosse Politik der Europäischen Kabinette, 1871-1914. Sammlung der Diplomatischen Akten des Auswärtigen Amtes. Im Auftrage des Auswärtigen Amtes herausgegeben von Johannes Lepsius, Albrecht Mendelssohn Bartholdy, Friedrich Thimme. Forty volumes. Berlin, 1922-27.

German Diplomatic Documents, 1871-1914. Selected and translated by E.T.S. Dugdale. Four volumes. London, 1928.

British Documents on the Origins of the War, 1898-1914. Edited by G. P. Gooch and Harold Temperley. Volumes I-IX, XI. London, 1926- .

Hansard Parliamentary Debates.

The Times. London.

Standard. London.

Norddeutsche Allgemeine Zeitung. Berlin.

MEMOIRS, LETTERS, SPEECHES, ETC.

English

George Macaulay Trevelyan: *The Life of John Bright.* London, 1913.

Sir Arthur Hardinge: *The Life of the Fourth Earl of Carnarvon.* Edited by Elizabeth Countess of Carnarvon. Three volumes. London, 1925.

J. L. Garvin: *The Life of Joseph Chamberlain.* Three volumes. London, 1932- .

Speeches of the Right Hon. Joseph Chamberlain, M.P. With a sketch of his life. Edited by Henry W. Lucy. London, 1885.

Mr. Chamberlain's Speeches. Edited by Charles W. Boyd. With an introduction by the Right Hon. Austen Chamberlain, M.P. Two volumes. London, 1914.

Speeches and Addresses of Edward Henry XVth Earl of Derby K.G. Selected and edited by Sir T. H. Sanderson, K.C.B., and E. S. Roscoe. With a prefatory memoir by W.E.H. Lecky. Two volumes. London, 1894.

Stephen Gwynn and Gertrude M. Tuckwell: *The Life of the Rt. Hon. Sir Charles W. Dilke, Bart., M.P.* Two volumes. London, 1917.

John Morley: *The Life of William Ewart Gladstone.* Three volumes. London, 1903.

Lord Edmond Fitzmaurice: *The Life of Granville George Leveson Gower, Second Earl Granville, K.G.* Two volumes. London, 1905.

A. G. Gardiner: *The Life of Sir William Harcourt.* Two volumes. London, 1923.

Sir Perceval Laurence, K.C.M.G.: *The Life of John Xavier Merriman.* London, 1930.

Basil Williams: *Cecil Rhodes.* London, 1921.

The Marquess of Crewe, K.G.: *Lord Rosebery.* Two volumes. London, 1931.

Lady Gwendolen Cecil: *Life of Robert Marquis of Salisbury.* Four volumes. London, 1921- .

Roundell Palmer, Earl of Selborne: *Memorials.* Two volumes. London, 1896 and 1898.

The Letters of Queen Victoria. Edited by George Earle Buckle: Second Series, three volumes, London, 1926-28; Third Series, three volumes, London, 1930-32.

German

Friedrich Ferdinand Graf von Beust: *Aus Drei Viertel-Jahrhunderten. Erinnerungen und Aufzeichnungen.* Two volumes. Stuttgart, 1887.

Wolfgang Windelband: *Herbert Bismarck als Mitarbeiter seines Vaters.* Berlin, 1921.

Ludwig Hahn and Carl Wippermann: *Fürst Bismarck, Sein politisches Leben und Wirken.* (Vollständige, pragmatisch geordnete Sammlung der Reden, Depeschen, Staatsschriften und politischen Briefe des Fürsten.) Five volumes. Berlin, 1878-91.

Fürst Bismarck als Redner. Vollständige Sammlung der parlamentarischen Reden Bismarcks seit dem Jahre 1847. Sachlich und chronologisch geordnet mit Einleitungen und Erläuterungen versehen von Wilhelm Böhm und Alfred Dove. Sixteen volumes. Stuttgart, 1885-91.

Bismarck: *Die Gesammelten Werke.* Edited by: Herman von Petersdorff; Friedrich Thimme; Werner Frauendienst; Willy Andreas; Wilhelm Schüssler; Wolfgang Windelband; Gerhard Ritter; Rudolf Stadelmann. Fifteen volumes. Berlin, 1924-35.

Moritz Busch: *Bismarck, Some Secret Pages of His History.* Three volumes. London, 1898.

Charles Lowe: *Prince Bismarck, An Historical Biography.* Two volumes. London, 1886.

Memoirs of Prince von Bülow. Translated from the German by Geoffrey Dunlop and F. A. Voigt. Four volumes. Boston, 1931-32.

Hermann Freiherr von Eckardstein: *Lebenserinnerungen und Politische Denkwürdigkeiten.* Three volumes. Leipzig, 1919-20.

Aus 50 Jahren. Erinnerungen, Tagebücher und Briefe aus dem Nachlass des Fürsten Philipp zu Eulenburg-Hertefeld. Berlin, 1923.

Memoirs of Prince Chlodwig of Hohenlohe-Schillingsfuerst. Two volumes. London, 1906.

Denkwürdigkeiten des General-Feldmarschalls Alfred Grafen von Waldersee. Auf Veranlassung des Generalleutnants Georg Grafen von Waldersee bearbeitet und herausgegeben von Heinrich Otto Meisner. Three volumes. Stuttgart, 1923.

GENERAL

Martin Aldao: *Les Idées Coloniales de Jules Ferry.* Paris, 1933.

C. A. Bodelsen: *Studies in Mid-Victorian Imperialism.* Copenhagen, 1924.

E. Bourgeois and G. Pagès: *Les Origines et les Responsabilités de la Grande Guerre.* Paris, 1921.

The Earl of Cromer: *Modern Egypt.* Two volumes. London, 1908.

Paul Darmstaedter: *Geschichte der Aufteilung und Kolonisation Afrikas.* Two volumes. Berlin, 1913 and 1920.

William Harbutt Dawson: *The Evolution of Modern Germany.* London, 1908.

____: *The German Empire, 1867-1914.* Two volumes. London, 1919.

Sir Charles W. Dilke: *Greater Britain.* London, 1868.

____: *Problems of Greater Britain.* London, 1890.

____: *The Present Position of European Politics, or Europe in 1887.* London, 1887.

James A. Froude: *Oceana, or England and Her Colonies.* London, 1886.

Joseph Vincent Fuller: *Bismarck's Diplomacy at Its Zenith.* Cambridge, Mass., 1922.

W. E. Gladstone: *England's Mission,* published in the *Nineteenth Century,* September 1878, Vol. IV, pp. 560-84.

____: *Kin Beyond Sea,* published in the *North American Review,* September-October 1878, Vol. CXXVII, pp. 179-212.

G. P. Gooch: *Franco-German Relations, 1871-1914.* London, 1928.

Maximilian von Hagen: *Bismarcks Kolonialpolitik.* Stuttgart, 1923.

____: *England und Ägypten, Materialen zur Geschichte der britischen Okkupation mit besonderer Rücksicht auf Bismarcks Ägyptenpolitik.* Bonn, 1915.

Otto Hammann: *Der Missverstandne Bismarck, Zwanzig Jahre Deutscher Weltpolitik.* Berlin, 1921.

Rudolf Ibbeken: *Das aussenpolitische Problem Staat und Wirtschaft in der deutschen Reichspolitik 1880-1914.* Schleswig, 1928.

J. Scott Keltie: *The Partition of Africa.* London, 1893.

Mathilde Kleine: *Deutschland und die Ägyptische Frage, 1875-1890.* Greifswald, 1927.

Paul Knaplund: *Gladstone and Britain's Imperial Policy.* New York, 1927.

____: *Gladstone's Foreign Policy.* New York, 1935.

Max von Koschitzky: *Deutsche Colonialgeschichte.* Two volumes. Leipzig, 1888.

William L. Langer: *European Alliances and Alignments, 1871-1890.* New York, 1931.

____: *The Diplomacy of Imperialism, 1890-1902.* Two volumes. New York, 1935.

Paul Leroy-Beaulieu: *De la Colonisation chez les Peuples Modernes*. Paris, 1874.

Reginald Ivan Lovell: *The Struggle for South Africa, 1875-1899. A Study in Economic Imperialism*. New York, 1934.

Alfred Milner: *England in Egypt*. London, 1892.

Parker Thomas Moon: *Imperialism and World Politics*. New York, 1926.

Hermann Oncken: *Das Deutsche Reich und die Vorgeschichte des Weltkrieges*. Two volumes. Leipzig, 1933.

Alfred Francis Pribram: *England and the International Policy of the European Great Powers, 1871-1914*. Oxford, 1931.

Felix Rachfahl: *Deutschland und die Weltpolitik, 1871-1914*. Band I, *Die Bismarck'sche Aera*. Stuttgart, 1923.

Helmuth Rogge: *Bismarcks Kolonialpolitik als aussenpolitisches Problem*, published in *Historische Vierteljahrschrift*, Vol. XXI, pp. 305-33 and 423-43.

Hans Rothfels: *Bismarcks englische Bündnispolitik*. Stuttgart, 1924.

Theodore Rothstein: *Egypt's Ruin, A Financial and Administrative Record*. With an introduction by Wilfrid Scawen Blunt. London, 1910.

J. R. Seeley: *The Expansion of England, Two Courses of Lectures*. London, 1883.

A History of the Peace Conference of Paris. Edited by H.W.V. Temperley. Six volumes. London, 1920-24.

Friedrich Thimme: *Das Memorandum E. A. Crowes vom 1. Januar 1907. Seine Bedeutung für die Kriegsschuldfrage*. Published in *Berliner Monatshefte*, Vol. VII, pp. 732-68, August 1929.

——: *Das "berühmte Schwindeldokument" E. A. Crowes*. Published in *Berliner Monatshefte*, Vol. VII, pp. 874-79, September 1929.

Mary Evelyn Townsend: *Origins of Modern German Colonialism, 1871-1885*. New York, 1921.

——: *The Rise and Fall of Germany's Colonial Empire, 1884-1918*. New York, 1930.

Robert H. Wienefeld: *Franco-German Relations, 1878-1885*. Baltimore, 1929.

Alfred Zimmermann: *Geschichte der Deutschen Kolonialpolitik*. Berlin, 1914.

INDEX

Africa, *see* South West Africa, Cameroons
Ampthill, Baron, (formerly Lord Odo Russell): 1, 16f., 19, 26, 82; failure of, to foresee German colonial policy, 41ff., 55f., 76f.; illness of, 43, 56; and Angra Pequena, 77ff., 86f., 89, 91, 94f., 101f., 108, 110, 116, 121f., 124, 144ff.
Angra Pequena, *see* South West Africa
Argyll, Duke of: opinion of Lord Granville, 130f.
Australian colonies: attempt of, to annex New Guinea, 11ff.

Bismarck, Count Herbert: 25, 28ff., 38f., 40f., 43, 79f., 147f.; visit of, to London in 1881, 1f., 16f., 156; mission of, in 1884, 89, 91-99, 101ff., 107-13, 118, 144ff., 150-53, 156f., 164; admits German views not clearly stated, 29, 92, 109; and penal settlement condition, 107f., 111f., 116f., 124; mission of, in 1885, 157, 160f.; character of, 91f., 154-62
Bismarck, Prince: 1f., 9f., 38f.; general foreign policy of, 3ff.; views of, on colonial policy, 18-27, 41ff.; and Angra Pequena, 28-34, 36f., 53ff., 57f., 59ff., 67ff., 72ff., 76f., 83-88, 90f., 93ff., 106ff., 110ff., 115ff., 121ff., 125-35, 144-53; efforts of, for general understanding with England, 52f., 61-64, 70ff.; secrecy of, 33, 67, 69, 82f., 90, 126ff., 133f., 148; and Egypt, 1f., 62, 89, 93ff., 113ff., 124, 132-35, 165ff.; relations with Count Herbert Bismarck, 154ff., 159-62
Bismarck, Count Wilhelm, 124, 161
Bleichröder, von, 161
Blue Books, British, 71, 93, 109, 126, 142-47, 152f.
Bojanowski, von, 32, 38f.
Bright, John, 10
British colonial office, *see* Derby, Herbert
British diplomacy: general character of, 3ff.; influence of imperialism on, 2, 4f.; Salisbury's views on, 3. *See* Granville, Gladstone, Derby, British foreign office.
British foreign office, *see* Granville, Pauncefote, Dallas, Currie
Bucher, Lothar, 156, 159f.
Bülow, Prince, 157, 159, 161
Busch, Klemens, 157
Busch, Moritz, 156f., 159f.

Cameroons: proposed annexation of, to England in 1882, 9; annexation of, by Germany in 1884, 9, 11
Cape Colony, 35f., 46-51, 65, 74f., 96f., 102-06, 117ff., 121f., 131, 134, 149. *See* Merriman, Robinson, Scanlen
Carnarvon, Earl of, 12f., 90
Carolath, Princess Elizabeth, 155
Chamberlain, Joseph: views of, on imperialism, 7, 10ff., 15, 137-41; disapproves of British policy, 126; and Majuba crisis, 137-41
Colonial office, British, *see* British colonial office
Currie, Sir Philip, 25f., 35, 40, 83

Dallas, Sir George, 60, 74, 78f., 83, 86f.
De Pass, Daniel, 34, 47, 103-06, 111
Derby, Earl of: 34, 39f., 69, 164, 166; views of, on imperialism, 2, 5, 7, 12ff.; susceptibility of, to colonial demands, 36, 103ff., 127ff.; and Angra Pequena, 44ff., 48-51, 60f., 65-68, 74, 76, 79, 90, 92, 94, 96, 98-106, 119f., 128-32, 143; encourages Cape Colony to annexation in South West Africa, 102-06, 117-21
Dilke, Sir Charles W.: 15f., 82, 94, 97, 156f.; imperialism of, 7ff., 15f.; disapproves of British policy, 126f.

Eckardstein, Baron von, 21
Egypt: England and, 1f., 62, 89, 93ff., 113ff., 124, 131-35, 165ff. *See* Bismarck, Granville, Münster
England, *see* British colonial office,

British diplomacy, British foreign office, Cape Colony, Egypt, Blue Books, Gladstone, Granville, Derby
Eulenburg, Prince, 155

Fabri, 23
Ferry, Jules, 114, 133ff.
Fiji Islands, 13, 19, 52f., 61, 99
Foreign office, British, *see* British foreign office
Foreign office, German, *see* German foreign office
France: and Egypt, 1f., 113ff., 132f.; and Germany, 132-35. *See* Ferry, Waddington, Egypt
Frankenberg, Count, 20
Frederick, Empress, 82, 158

German foreign office, *see* Prince Bismarck, Count Herbert Bismarck, Hatzfeldt, Klemens Busch, Bojanowski, Holstein, Rantzau
Germany: growth of population and emigration in, 21; economic changes in, 21f., 27; explorers of, 22f.; missionaries of, 23; colonial movement in, 23ff.; commerce of, in Africa and South Seas, 24f. *See* Bismarck, German foreign office, White Books, South West Africa, Cameroons, New Guinea
Gladstone, William Ewart: 88, 130f., 137, 158; anti-imperialism of, 2, 5ff., 12, 14ff., 17, 164f.; relations of, with cabinet, 15f.; and German colonial question, 100f., 133, 163-68
Granville, Earl: 1, 3f., 16f., 25, 31, 44, 53, 69f., 130f., 156f., 163; and Angra Pequena, 29, 34, 36, 40f., 43, 60, 66, 73-76, 79, 83, 86, 89f., 92-112, 119f., 130, 143-46, 150-53, 164f.; and penal settlement condition, 102, 106ff., 115ff.; and Egypt, 93ff., 113ff., 124, 132-35; effect of colonial incident on, 130f.

Hagen, Maximilian von, 156f., 161
Harcourt, Sir William: anti-imperialism of, 2, 7, 15; disapproves of British policy, 99f.
Hartington, Marquis of, 127
Hatzfeldt, Count, 38f., 41f., 67, 69, 77f., 82, 84f., 87, 103, 108, 118ff., 154, 159
Heligoland, 62ff., 68, 71, 73
Herbert, Sir Robert G. W., 31, 35
Hohenlohe, Prince, 20, 157f., 161
Holstein, Baron von, 157, 159
Hoyos, Countess Margarete, 154
Hübbe-Schleiden, 23

Kimberley, Earl of, 44, 94, 100
Kleinmichel, Countess, 157
Kusserow, Heinrich von, 53f., 57f.

Lippert, 33f., 39, 47, 52, 55, 57, 68f., 103, 118f., 148
List, Friedrich, 23
Lüderitz, F. A. E.: proposes German colony in Transvaal, 19; and Angra Pequena, 27f., 30-33, 37, 38f., 54, 59, 69, 83, 85, 101, 104, 117, 143, 148

Malet, Sir Edward, 20, 71, 125f.
Merriman, John X., 47, 50
Münster, Count: 4, 26, 52f., 59, 61-64, 160; character of, 81f.; and Angra Pequena, 31, 35ff., 38, 40f., 43, 69f., 75f., 89ff., 97f., 103, 108, 110f., 115f., 118, 122, 143-53; misconception of Bismarck's policy, 29, 41, 63ff., 71ff., 79ff., 125ff., 134; uninformed about Bismarck's plans, 67, 82-88, 127f., 134; and Egypt, 113ff.

New Guinea, 11ff., 100f., 160, 163
New Zealand, 13
Northbrook, Earl of, 2, 7, 17, 100

Pauncefote, Sir Julian, 30f., 38, 69, 74f., 78f., 86f., 104f., 109, 111, 119
Plessen, Baron von, 34, 118ff., 123, 142, 145, 150, 152
Plessen, Count, 1
Potter, T. B., advocates annexation in New Guinea, 12

Rantzau, Count, 159
Robinson, Sir Hercules, 48ff., 56f., 60, 83, 103ff.
Roebuck, J. A., on object of colonization, 6
Roon, Count von, 18f.
Roscher, Wilhelm, 23
Rosebery, Earl of, 88, 140, 158ff.
Rothfels, Hans, 161

Salisbury, Marquis of: views of, on British diplomacy, 3

Scanlen, Thomas, 35f., 48, 60, 75, 103, 129, 143
Selborne, Earl of: views of, on colonial annexations, 2, 7, 12f., 15
Sidmouth, Viscount: questions of, in House of Lords, 64ff., 73, 90
South West Africa: Angra Pequena, *see* Bismarck, Lüderitz, Granville, Derby, Ampthill, Münster
Spence, J., 47, 69, 85

Victoria, Queen, 130f.

Vitzthum, Count, 55

Waddington, William, 114
Waldersee, Count von, 158-61
Wales, Prince of, (Edward VII), 81f., 158
Weber: proposes German colony in Transvaal, 19
White Books, German, 28ff., 31, 33f., 38f., 69ff., 85f., 126, 134, 142, 145-53
Wolf, Eugen, 21